Your Real Estate Appraisal

The Industry Today and What Every Homeowner Should Know

Adrian Watts

Introduction

Real estate markets have been turbulent. Years of increasing values followed by declining markets have led the mortgage industry to be cautious. Consequently extensive guidelines apply to all sections of loan applications and the real estate appraisal report is no exception. In today's market the appraisal report is more complex than ever before.

Most of us will encounter the work of a real estate appraiser at some point in our lives. The result could be completely uneventful and hopefully so, but problems may arise. What happens if the property's appraised value is lower than expected? In some cases a buyer will have to renegotiate the contract. If a homeowner has applied to refinance they may move forward but with a higher interest rate. In other situations the loan may be denied due to insufficient collateral. The appraisal process is complicated, certainly expensive, and sadly sometimes leads to no result.

This text discusses the appraisal process and all its facets as they relate to the mortgage industry at large. A borrower applying for a loan should know how this may affect them. It is better to know beforehand if there is going to be problem, or at least understand why the appraised value was unexpectedly low. The industry is not perfect and the appraiser has limitations on what they can or cannot do. Some limitations may cause borrowers to be frustrated: market practices, a lack of data to support any other value and restrictive Lender guidelines are examples. But in some cases *we* do make mistakes, and it would be helpful for the borrower to identify them and have some options to find a resolution. The average reader should be able to understand an appraisal report, at least to the point where it makes sense. Unfortunately there are too many incidences of appraisers writing reports that are confusing even for experienced eyes.

Due to recent market stabilizations and increases, homeowners wishing to refinance have high expectations about their property value. A loan officer will ask the borrower, during the early stages of refinancing, for an estimate of their property value. Homeowners need to think long and hard before answering this question. Research is necessary and the answer has to be as conservative as possible. Too many homeowners do not accomplish their goals, or realize the expected saving on their loan because of misjudgments.

What happens when the appraisal process fails? Reality dictates that sometimes things go wrong! Today, if there is a valuation issue, too low, the Lender has little leeway on what they can do. Traditionally speaking it was at the Lender's discretion, why and when a second appraisal was ordered and they did it frequently. The system was open to abuse and indeed was. In response, since the fall of 2011, the delivery of every appraisal report is accompanied by an electronic record. The system has practically eliminated the possibility of a second try, which was its intent. Lenders have protocols for a suspected over-valuation and these have remained fairly constant. But for an under-valuation there is no system to deal with deficient appraisals. Homeowners have the options of rebutting the appraisal report and in some rare cases when it is obviously deficient the appraisal might be re-ordered. Going to another Lender, which would require the additional expense of paying for another appraisal, might be an option. Even then this possibility is eliminated when applying for a FHA and some conventional financing without first undergoing a waiting period. Essentially in today's market a home-owner has one chance.

There are millions of people who live and work in the whole industry and rely on a professional valuation. Buying a property will involve most of the following parties: real estate agent, loan officer, appraiser, surveyor, property inspectors (home, environmental or structural), title agents, mortgage insurers, mortgage banker, and bank and then the end investor.

The complete appraisal, which contains all field notes, worksheets, data, sketches and listings, is retained by the appraiser. The appraisal report everyone sees is a <u>summary</u> of the complete appraisal. Even though the Lender orders the appraisal, the homeowner should have a reasonable expectation of quality. It is their property after all.

This text relates only to real estate appraisals for the mortgage industry at large and includes those appraisals that will be sold on and secondary markets, such as Fannie Mae and Freddie Mac. Even though these two, known as the (GSE's), are responsible for purchasing the largest number of mortgage loans, the secondary market is expansive and has many players. For appraisal purposes their guidelines may vary but the essential core "GSE" guidelines are the most significant. Fannie Mae is referenced many times within this text. Appraisers use the term "Fannie Mae" as a synonym for the Secondary Market and we will also use it where relevant.

Throughout the text there are bolded segment of information. These highlights check the most common issues a borrower might be concerned with for each topic.

What is an Appraisal?

An appraisal of real property is a legal document meant to support the collateral part of a loan. The document is ordered by the Lender as part the mortgage process and is paid for by the borrower. Despite this, and to clear up a commonly asked question, the appraisal report is the property of the Lender and not the borrower.

The appraisal in the mortgage industry is reported on a series of forms with addenda depending on property type. These forms create the backbone to every report and are:

a) URAR Single family homes; detached and attached including modular homes.

b) Small Residential Income Property. Used for 2-4 rental units only.

c) Condominium. Used for anything with a legal condominium status. Property types include may townhomes on common land, site condominiums and landominiums.

d) Manufactured Homes.

In addition to the main form residential appraisal reports are delivered with a Market Conditions Report (MCR); a form meant to analyze current market value trends and report on current levels of foreclosures. This form is one to remember and pertinent in segments of several discussions within this text. There are other forms issued by Government Agencies or Lenders, but only play a limited role and not found in the majority of appraisal reports. The appraisal report also comes with written addenda explaining the data presented in the form and the appraiser's disclosures. The majority of the remaining pages in the average report, however, which ranges from 25-50 pages, are additional addenda, consisting of photos of the subject's exterior and interior, location and aerial maps, plus any additional client requested addenda. The latter may include anything from copies of appraiser's licenses, on occasion copies of errors and omissions policies and lists of available sales in the area. The complete appraisal report is a lengthy document.

Each form is structured with each section labeled in black is the left. For the single family home these sections are: subject, contract, neighborhood, site, improvements, sales comparison, reconciliation, additional comments, cost approach, income and PUD information. These section are referenced many times.

The appraisal report being a legal document has an assignee, which for mortgage purposes is the Lender and maybe FHA, but never the borrower. An assignee must have a designated use for the appraisal report. A borrower has no legal use, in this context, and therefore is not an assignee; appraisers call assignees the intended user. In this case the intended user is the Lender and the intended use for the appraisal report is mortgage purposes. A homeowner may not take an appraisal report with the intended use for mortgage purposes and use it for anything else. For example, to use the report to settle an estate will require a new appraisal with the intended use "for estate purposes" and the names of the attorneys and relevant parties as intended users. A Lender may also not use an appraisal report prepared for a different Lender without first getting permission from the borrower to have their name removed as the intended user (see appraiser certification #21 in the fine print). The new Lender will have to go back to the appraiser and show they are now the intended user with a new appraisal report produced.

Check #1. When comparing two appraisal reports ensure that the intended <u>uses</u> are comparable. Borrowers may read the appraisal even though they are not a user. One must have an "intended use" to be an "intended user". Reading and even criticizing is not an intended use.

The appraisal is an estimate of value according to the current definition of market value. The definition of market value varies, according to what the appraisal is being used for. For example the definition of liquidation value is going to differ from a regular sale. A regular sale would be exposed to the marketplace having time to reach its market value while a liquidation sales' value lies in an immediate payable price. A homeowner needs to read the report in its entirety, but if not then at least the definition of market value which is fundamental to the whole appraisal process. For mortgage purposes per Fannie Mae is definition is:

Market value is the most probable price which a property should bring in a competitive and open market under all conditions requisite to a fair sale, the buyer and seller, each acting prudently, knowledgeably and assuming the price is not affected by undue stimulus.

This definition is included in the report usually on page 4 of the single family and condominium forms (or 5 for multi 2-4 units) titled "Definition of Market Value". The text is on the first page of the small print after the data presentation. The definition is further clarified via:

Implicit in this definition is the consummation of a sale as of a specified date and the passing of title from seller to buyer under conditions whereby: (1) buyer and seller are typically motivated; (2) both parties are well informed or well advised, and each acting in what he or she considers his or her own best interest; (3) a reasonable time is allowed for exposure in the open market; (4) payment is made in terms of cash in U. S. dollars or in terms of financial arrangements comparable thereto; and (5) the price represents the normal consideration for the property sold unaffected by special or creative financing or sales concessions granted by anyone associated with the sale.

This operative phrase in this definition is "probable value". This means the value which is closest to "true value". This is an adjusted value and technically speaking assumes the adjustments to find true value are correct. Unfortunately this is not necessarily the value seen in some appraisal reports. This is because the mortgage industry, being encumbered in Lender guidelines, is more conservative in terms of valuations and especially since the markets declines from 2006 onwards. In respect to the accuracy of valuations it is worth reiterating the appraisal process is filled with limitations and subjectivity making "probable value" hard to achieve.

Not referred to in this definition of market value, and crucial to Lenders is the subject's *marketability*. Every property has a value, but not every property is immediately marketable, something a Lender needs in case of borrower default. The subject's overall marketability, as of the effective date of evaluation, plays a role in what a homebuyer is also willing to pay. Properties with superior marketability do sell for higher than median prices.

The Lender is interested in anything that may affect the subject's marketability and the chapter -Things that _May_ Kill the Deal- covers most concerns. Establishing these elements behind value is critical to understanding what an appraisal is, in the eyes of the Lender. After all, their main goal is to minimize risk. It is not uncommon for appraisers to add the tag line, when referring to a specific feature in a property, "and does not affect marketability" with this being a reflection of Lender's concern.

The appraisal "form" does not specifically ask for a description or question the subject's overall marketability but reporting this correctly is an exceptionally pertinent part of the overall report. It is assumed that the appraiser will address any pertinent factors. Interestingly while negative marketability factors are usually reported, positive ones are not.

Check #2. Does the report accurately describe the subject's marketability including any positive factors? These could be: school districts, nearby parks and recreation, views, energy efficient items and easy access or walking distance to retail shopping areas and commuter transportation.

How does an Appraiser form an Opinion of Value?

In valuation a similar set of principles apply, be it appraising a house or an antique. Anyone that has watched the antiques road show will know only a range of values is offered for Grandma's vase and never a specific value. The appraiser quotes between $8,000-$12,000 and not $10,000. Yet valuations in the mortgage industry always have a specific value. The Lender must have a figure to base loan amounts from and therefore a range in value would be useless. But real estate appraisers cannot do much more than the guy appraising Grandma's vase, so in the mortgage industry appraisers use their judgment and reason to determine a specific value. This is the most subjective part of the appraisal process but whatever the result is, it has to be deemed reasonable, make sense and is explained.

The appraisal process can be summarized in five steps. These are; defining the problem, setting a scope of work, collecting data, analyzing data and finally the reconciliation of that data. The last process, reconciliation is where the appraiser reviews the data and chooses a number in that range -see How a Reconciliation reads?

Most likely the appraiser will try to complete steps one and two, defining the problem and assessing the scope of work, when considering whether to accept the appraisal assignment. Assignments can be more problematic than they appear! Less experienced appraisers make frequent errors in underestimating the scope of work. In fact this happens to everyone on occasion and is sometimes inevitable. If incorrect information is provided in either the appraisal order or public sources, the definition of the problem and scope of work are not set correctly and will have to be reconsidered. Usually this will not discovered until setting the appointment or even at the property. Nowadays with mobile internet access this problem can be remedied immediately. Professional appraisal standards recommend the appraiser to be flexible in the scope of work. There is evidence, however that some appraisers complete the assignment under their original scope of work despite information uncovered in the appraisal process that should alter it.

Step three is collecting data, and by the time of the appointment the appraiser normally has a good idea of any possible sales they could use for comparison to the subject. Field data is collected during the inspection and reviewed with the previously selected sales to see if they are still applicable. This is because there are variances between online sources and information provided by homeowners or real estate agents. After the inspection the appraiser begins asking a series of questions. For example- *Are these sales truly comparable?* and *Do they have similar features and finishes?* Appraisers then pair down the sales "comparables" or "comps" to those they consider the most viable and follow that with an exterior inspection. During the drive-by the appraiser should also be observant of any possible variances between online data and for the comparable sale. If there are significant variances an appraiser showing good standards will adjust the scope of work.

As indicated there is a segment of the profession that can form an early opinion as to which sales are indicators of value for the subject. Typically this is realized too late, the appraisal is written and already in dispute. Possible verbal signs of this are comments similar to "I was certain when I left that house" or "The instant I walked in…" and "I pulled 6 comps beforehand", none of which bode well. In addition the comparable sales data used in the report can show a lack of flexible work procedures, especially if the gross living area (GLA) of all comparables is noticeably more similar to an incorrect online GLA for the subject. The availability of sales is easily verifiable and that will reveal if there is a problem.

Check #3. A homeowner should compare the gross living area (GLA) in the appraisal report to online sources (the assessor). Disparities are frequent between field data and online sources. When it comes to GLA it is common for an appraiser to measure a greater square footage in the field.

The last two steps of the appraisal process are analyzing the data and a reconciliation of that data. Each comparable sale is adjusted which offers a range in values. From this an actual opinion of value is taken and the reconciliation is the explanation. After completing all five steps, then and only then, is the appraisal compete.

Understanding an Appraisal

Perhaps the answer is "Isn't that what we are all trying to work out?" Frivolous comments aside the appraisal industry always had a problem with varying reporting standards. The variance makes it difficult for secondary market Lenders to analyze their portfolios. Analysts would find it challenging to understand the variety of reporting methods from across the country to perform quality control. In response, during the fall of 2011, Fannie Mae and Freddie Mac (GSE's) introduced the Uniform Appraisal Dataset (UAD). The idea behind this was to standardize responses to questions and conditions throughout the report in an effort to enhance appraisal quality and consistency. The GSE's did not ask for this standard to be applied to every property type, with 2-4 multi units and manufactured homes excluded. UAD is outlined in 37 pages but a summary is included as a three page addenda in all single family and condominium reports. The addendum summarizes the respective quality and condition ratings for the property. These are denoted as "Q", for quality of construction, and "C" for condition respectively in the sales grid. A scale from 1 to 6 is used to rate the subject and comparable sales. C1 indicates new construction and Q1 a high quality of construction. Q5-6 and C5-6 mean there is significant deferred maintenance and most Lenders will not accept properties with either of these classifications without remedy. Also in the three page addenda is a list of the remaining abbreviations and definitions which cover practically every appraisal related circumstance. This second set of abbreviations set can be coupled together in the report as often seen in the site section or sales grid. For example "N:Res" is two abbreviations meaning the subject has a neutral and residential location. The list is quite extensive, and also includes abbreviations for types of sales which is used in the contract section. Here it is stated if the transaction, if applicable, is arm's length or not. An arm's length sales is typically the result of the subject being exposed to the market, while a non arms length sale would have no exposure to the market and for example could a sale between relatives.

The side by side comparison of the subject and sales is referred to as the sales grid. This is found on page 2 of the single family form and page 3 of the condominium and 2-4 multi unit form. Most readers focus on the sales grid when trying to understand an appraisal.

Check #4. The property ratings in the grid, "Q" and "C" should be relevant to the property in question. The appraiser's opinions of quality and condition have to be consistent. In other words if a remodeled home is described as C2, then all comparables with the condition rating C2, also need to be remodeled. Do the other abbreviations used describe the property accurately?

The sales grid contains variations between the subject and sales. If no adjustment is due to account for the variance a zero is placed next to the variance. Below is a sample of the Comparable Sales grid.

FEATURE	SUBJECT	COMPARABLE SALE #1		COMPARABLE SALE #2		COMPARABLE SALE #3	
Address 127 Gilberts Rd, Canaryville, IA		358 Preston St, Canaryville, IA		759 Norton Way, Canaryville, IA		129 Hammond Ln, Canaryville IA	
Proximity to Subject		0.27 Miles NW		0.57 Miles SW		1.35 miles	
Sales Price	295,000		292,300		327,400		274,500
Sales Price/GLA	$ 125.00	$ 125.50		$ 118.02		$ 126.49	
Data Sources		LNLS #678142		LNLS #677100		LNLS # 677569	
Verification Source(s)		Assessor/Exterior Inspection		Assessor/Exterior Inspection		Assessor/Exterior Inspection	
VALUE ADJUSTMETS	DESCRIPTION	DESCRIPTION	+ (-) Adj'ment	DESCRIPTION		DESCRIPTION	+ (-) Adj'ment
Sales or Financing Concessions		Arms Length FHA $ 4000	-4000	Arms Length Conv None	0	Arms Length Conv None	0
Date of Sales/Time	9/26/2012	S:07/12,C:05/12		S:07/12,C:08/12		S:02/12,C:04/12	
Location	Suburban	Suburban		Suburban		Suburban	
Leasehold/Fee Simple	Fee Simple	Fee Simple		Fee Simple		Fee Simple	
Site	14,750	12,570		10,490	2000	19,500	-3000
View	N:Res	N:Res		N:Res		N:Res	
Design (Style)	Colonial	Colonial		Colonial		Colonila	
Quality of Construction	Q2	Q2		Q2		Q3	-4000
Actual Age	17	23	0	10		33	-4000
Condition	C3	C3		C3		C4	6000
Above Grade	Total Beds Bths	Total Beds Bths		Total Beds Bths		Total Beds Bths	
Room Count	9 3 2.1	8 3 2.1	-7000	8 4 3.1	-7000	8 3 2.1	
Gross Living Area	2424	2329	4800	2774	-10,500	2170	7600
Basement	1127sf817sfwu	1117sf517sfwu	0	1350sf1217sfw	-4500	1100sf400sfwu	2500
Fin Rms Below Grade	1rr0br1,0ba1o	1rr1br0,0ba0o	5000	1rr0br1,0ba1o		1rr0br0,0ba0o	6000
Functional Utility	Avg 3 Bedrooms	Avg 3 Bedrooms		Avg 4 Bedrooms	-4000	Avg 3 Bedrooms	
Heating/Cooling	F-Air/CAC	F-Air/CAC		F-Air/CAC		F-Air/CAC	
Energy Efficient Items	Typ for Market	Typ for Market		Typ for Market		Typ for Market	
Garage/Carport	2 Cat Att	2 Cat Att		3 Cat Att	-5000	2 Cat Att	
Porch/Patio/Deck	Deck	Patio	1000	Deck /Patio	-2000	Patio	1000
Fireplace	One	None	-2000	Two	-2000	Two	-2000
Net Adjustment (Total)		☒ + ☐ -	$	☐ + ☒ -	$	☒ + ☐ -	$
Adjusted Sales Price of Comparables		Net Adj. 1.8 % Gross Adj. 4.6 %	$297,800	Net Adj. 8.8% Gross Adj. 10.7	$298,400	Net Adj. 9.8% Gross Adj. 13.6	$290,620

Having some knowledge of how the grid works is valuable. In theory the very top area of the grid under the comparable sales address is the most important information, and includes the conditions of sale, arms length and type of sales and then either fee simple or leasehold. The next two lines are given to the subject's site and then the subject's characteristics. After that each features' relevance diminishes going down the column. The basement line is also called the "base-line" and it is typical to have any adjustment above the base-line explained in the report. The appraiser also has three additional lines to use at the very bottom of the grid for additional items.

Check # 5. Watch out for last minute modernization adjustments placed on the last three lines of the grid. These adjustments could be for superior kitchens or bathrooms. Ask if these adjustments are applicable and even though they are below the base-line they should be explained.

The description of bathrooms is formatted with the number of full baths first, followed by the number of half baths. For example 1.2 baths equals, one full bath and two half baths. Basement bathrooms are reported separately on the line below with the other basement finished areas. A bath must have a minimum of three elements, tub and/or a shower, sink and commode to be a full bath. A half bath consists of any two elements. There is no such thing as a quarter bath in the eyes of an appraiser.

Laundry, mud-rooms, foyers and baths are not counted in the total room count.

Common Appraisal Mistakes

Field appraisers are people and we all make mistakes. The average report may have many simple errors most of which are resolved in quality control. Within appraisal reports inconsistencies between the written text and the data, or conflicts within the data itself are common. Other sets of "mistakes" arise from differing regions of the country and another group which derive themselves from what education the appraiser has had. A regional variance in ideas is acceptable, but by all accounts nothing in the report should conflict with either good appraisal practice or standard appraisal theory.

Appraiser education also plays a role with who mentored them, what classes they took and who they worked for, which all contribute to varying opinions. Mentors can hand down erroneous beliefs, and occasionally instructors come up with quirky opinions during continuing education classes. In addition an appraiser might get into bad habits working for a substandard company. All these circumstances lead to problems which are difficult to solve, as this is what the appraiser was taught and therefore believes. In fact some of these appraisal reporting practices may be acceptable for other intended users, but not for the typical Lender and expectations of today's secondary market.

Lenders can be over reaching in their guidelines. Some appraisers will complete a report in strict accordance with the engagement letter. In areas of declining markets most Lenders still ask for two sales within three months. Numerous other Lenders, in these times of more stable markets still ask for sales within six months. The result is fundamental appraisal principles, like location and similarity, being set aside in preference to when a particular property sold simply to fulfill Lender guidelines.

Appraisers typically receive only 48 hours after inspection to return the report and this limited window also contributes to human error in the preparation of the report. This lack of time partially accounts for errors and appraisal reports missing explanations to important points.

These are the circumstances behind common mistakes technical or otherwise. Common sources for additional errors result from: the quality of data, poor field data collection, and data entry.

The remainder of this discussion will concentrate on common technical errors. Some deserve their own chapters, so the essence is explained, and expanded on at a later time. In a report some mistakes are easily identifiable and some are not.

Check # 6. When reading through a report, observe the overall consistency. Discrepancies, above minor, are considered to discredit the report. Discrepancies are the most common of errors, and if co-existing with other errors can lead to questionable results.

Analysis of Market Conditions

Poor analysis of market conditions is a common error that creates a ripple effect throughout the subsequent analysis. It is often felt that the opinion of market conditions is formulated on insufficient data sets. An incorrect opinion of current markets doesn't allow the appraiser to proceed with a credible opinion of value thereafter. A chapter has been dedicated to the analysis of markets.

Adjustments

How the comparables are adjusted, and the adjusted amounts always seem to hold some questions, even controversy. They cause contention with the reader, but the appraiser is not able to apply every adjustment based on factual data if it does not exist. Some adjustments are completely subjective and some may only have an element of subjectivity, again depending on available data. Therefore in most cases an adjustment is largely the appraiser's opinion. When an adjustment ceases to be reasonable, does not make sense, and would not be supported by peers, it can be questioned. Most sales comparison approaches (the sales grid) are filled with a lively bunch of numbers. Some of them will matter and some will not.

Adjustments are created by crunching numbers, and combining them with market knowledge. When it comes to some adjustments, appraisers can "pop in a number" relying entirely on their market knowledge. Adjusting with no data, for major adjustments leads to questions if the value is the most "probable". Utility, gross living area (GLA), age, and lot size are all examples of major adjustments. There may be no other option, and if this is the case check the adjustments make sense, are proportional with property values and also the remaining adjustments. As stated, adjustments above the base-line should be explained.

Geographical area may also play a role on how a property is adjusted. There are patterns that exist between States, and between the subject's and appraiser's location be it either, rural, suburban or urban. For example, an urban appraiser valuing a suburban property with a well and septic would make a negative adjustment when comparing it to properties with public water and sewer. On the other hand, a rural appraiser valuing the same property most likely will not. The two appraisers view well and septic systems very differently, as the rural appraiser considers them typical while the urban or even suburban appraiser does not. In another instance, how appraisers consider a bi-level is split pretty much half and half in some States. Some include the below grade level area with the above grade GLA, while others separate the two in accordance with the typical appraisal practice for their area. In conclusion appraisers can have a range of opinions on the same subject within the same market and not all can be correct.

Check # 7. Look over some of the adjustments in the appraisal report. Are they proportional to the actual value and to the variances in values among the sales? For example is the appraiser adjusting a mere $5000 for an extra garage space on $500,000 property and if so why?

Homeowners frequently see low adjustments or the complete lack of adjustments, when one is apparently warranted. If an appraiser is questioned typical written responses are, "Data is too limited to extract an adjustment" or, "The market does not react to that feature". This is the appraiser's opinion which has to be respected. Nonetheless the reader should question the validity of that argument. Maybe this is the result of a lack of analysis, lack of time, or even skill on behalf of the appraiser. In certain circumstances one will never know. Hard data is needed to change an appraiser's opinion and even then good luck. In all cases it is hard for homeowners to accept low and absent adjustments. Better explanations from the appraiser than the above mentioned platitudes are due.

Appraisers tend not to adjust between numbers of bedrooms. Homeowners find this frustrating, as that extra bedroom adds to the homes functional utility in their eyes. Which of these two similar houses would you choose? Property A, with 3 bedrooms at $295,000, or property B with four bedrooms at $300,000. In addition quick interviews among the neighborhood public would verify there is a benefit in the extra bedroom, especially for younger families. Yet there are appraisers that state, there is no value in having an extra bedroom. It may indeed be a fact that there is no identifiable market reaction, but in many circumstances for properties in urban and suburban markets this is questionable. This is especially true between two and three bedrooms and the lack of this adjustment is frustrating. Market reaction between three and four bedroom homes would be less identifiable in most markets but again a family would pay extra for it. Within the grid there a separate line for functional utility where the appraiser can adjust for the number of bedrooms or other functional issues. Adjustment for functional utility are under-utilized, and their absence remains the most difficult to understand, as in many cases an adjustment would be supportable. Other items that frequently receive no adjustments are land, quality of construction and seller concessions, and each are discussed in their own context.

Borrowers may read through the sales grid and notice some items are adjusted for while others are not. This inconsistency is disliked and hard to understand, but in many ways this is a testament to the subjectivity of appraising. Nonetheless the practice appears a contradiction. For example, the appraiser has chosen not to adjust for items that create value, land or quality of construction and goes to great length to explain why. On the other hand, appraisers are happy to adjust for a fireplace or patio, being not only minor but very subjective items.

Check #8. See if the adjustments in the grid are consistent. For example if a half bath is adjusted at $3,000 then check this amount is consistent among the comparables. Similarly calculate the amount adjusted for GLA per square foot. Subject is 2,400 sq. ft and comparable 1 is 2,000 sq ft adjusted for GLA by $16000. 2400-2000=400 and 16000/ 400= $40 per square foot. This number should be compared to the total price per square foot of each comparable.

There are neighborhoods which do not consist of homogenous housing stock. Therefore the sales selected for comparison would be dissimilar from the subject and logically speaking lead to large adjustments. Not so, as appraisers all too often address these large variances with minimal adjustments. This gives the reader a wide range of adjusted values to consider. It is possible the adjustments are the only ones supportable given the available data, and therefore this is the best achievable outcome. This is an acceptable argument as one cannot expect what is not possible! However this creates the need for an explanation as to why each sale was included and a detailed reconciliation of adjusted values.

Fannie Mae gives appraisers guidelines for the sum of all adjustments. The total of all adjustments to any comparable sale price should not exceed 25%. Since some adjustments are positive and some negative, the difference should not exceed 15% of any comparable sale price. For example if a $100,000 house was adjusted +$5,000 for not having an extra bath, and -$5,000 for having an extra garage space, then the net adjustments are zero and the gross adjustments are 10%. In addition no single adjustment line should exceed 10% of the comparables sales price. Again there are some appraisers who will conform to Fannie guidelines, even when appraising a property in a neighborhood of non homogenous housing stock. What may occur is the appraiser squeezes the adjustments to conform to guidelines, which also leaves a large range on values. Fannie Mae put forth these as guidelines only and nothing more. These guidelines can be exceeded and must be when necessary.

There are some other observable patterns existing in the average sales grid within the sets of adjustments. Some items are traditionally under adjusted for while others are over adjusted. Items that are under adjusted for are gross living area (GLA), especially for condominiums, basements and land. On the other hand property condition adjustments often appear over adjusted. An adjustment has to be deemed reasonable and like everything make sense.

Sales Resulting from Foreclosures

Sales of foreclosed properties are termed "REO" sales. REO stands for "Real Estate Owned" and refers to properties that have been foreclosed upon and now are owned by the Lender. If the appraiser uses REOs as comparables sales to formulate even a part of the valuation it can make a difference in the opinion of value. There are few guidelines when it comes to the correct use of REO sales but some conventional wisdom exists. Typically if the neighborhood shows a foreclosure rate of 10% but no more than 15%, then no REO sales are included for comparison purposes. Above that and for a foreclosure rate between 15%-20%, max 25% then one REO sale should be included. This REO sale represents a base-line value for the Lender and its relevance is noted in the reconciliation. A foreclosure rate above 25% will likely indicate that values in the neighborhood are affected and it is up to the appraiser to assess that effect.

Description of Property

The appraisal report should, despite being just a summary, be something like a story with a beginning, middle and an end. The subject property is the main character and no amount of photographs can substitute for a good property description. Quality of materials used, aspects that would increase marketability, comments on wear and tear, functionality of floor plan would all be examples of points to include. Appraisal reports are frequently delivered without an adequate description of property or none at all. Fannie Mae guidelines ask for a description of the property so technically speaking a property description should always be included.

Sketches

A sketch of the property is provided with every appraisal. One would think this is a fairly straight forward process, but no. Mistakes result from all sorts of avenues and are relatively common. The range of possible sketch errors result from: simply not measuring the property at all or incorrectly, transcribing field notes incorrectly, using the assessor's website for exterior dimensions, copying the online sketch incorrectly, using incorrect building plans and the incorrect use of measuring devices. Measurements taken at the time of inspection determine gross living area (GLA) which is the most important piece of data appraisers collects and this needs to be accurate.

A sketch should include exterior measurements and the mathematics behind how each area and floor level is calculated. There are maybe a few accepted variances to condominiums (regional) but sketches are usually completed to Lender guidelines. A variance of 100 sq. ft between the appraiser's measurements and public sources is common for the typical property. For larger houses a variance of 5% is acceptable. Note that appraisers typically do not adjust for the first 100 sq. ft difference in GLA (referring to the average single family home of 1800 sq. ft plus and not condominiums) between the subject and comparables. One reason is to take in account the natural variance in data. This is basically an acknowledgement that the GLA numbers collected by the appraiser and assessor is not a perfect data-set and is an accepted strategy from a statistical point of view. There are exceptions noted below.

Check #9. Due to their commonality, check for mistakes in the sketch. Mistakes would be obvious and measured in feet rather than inches. The person most likely to notice a sketch error is the homeowner. Measure the property if necessary.

Functional Utility

An appraiser refers to functional utility in terms of number of bedrooms and baths followed by the total number of rooms. Most appraisers do not adjust for the total number of rooms a home has, but the number of rooms varies in terms of importance. In a contemporary property the number of rooms is irrelevant. In traditional style homes, notably Victorian, the total number of rooms does matter. More rooms may not be better in older homes. If the subject and some comparables have seven rooms, while one comparable has eleven rooms it might indicate a lack of remodeling for that sale. This is more of a concern for middle to high valued neighborhoods.

Appraisers frequently state the number of rooms is adjusted together with GLA, and this is acceptable but there is, at least one exception. Consider a small six room house, maybe 1100 sq ft with three bedrooms, dining room of 9ft x13ft (117 sq. ft) and a similar property, 1010 sq ft, five rooms, three bedrooms with no dining room. A homebuyer will choose the house with the dining room almost every time and probably pay a little extra as well. Adjustments for dining rooms are rarely made in appraisal reports for any property type. In addition the appraiser most likely will not adjust for less than 100 sq. ft difference in GLA anyway so the benefit of the dining room is completely lost in the valuation.

Appraisers always adjust for baths which is a product of convention. Technically speaking a bath adjustment would be one of the harder adjustments to analyze. The adjustments for baths seen in most report are not analyzed and usually subjective.

Seller Concessions

In essence, seller paid concessions are monies paid to facilitate the deal ensuring certain buyer costs will be covered by the seller at closing. The tool of including seller concessions in a contract is common practice. Typically the concession for each sale is deducted from the comparables sales price. Not all appraisers deduct for seller concessions and once again there are geographical variances.

The question remains when to adjust for seller concessions. At the end of the definition of market value, Fannie Mae clarifies when seller concessions should be adjusted for. It states:

"No adjustments are necessary for those costs which are normally paid by sellers as a result of tradition or law in a market area; these costs are readily identifiable since the seller pays these costs in virtually all sales transactions".

It would be nice to know what Fannie Mae means by *virtually all transactions* but it's reasonable to think they mean the vast majority. This means if seller concessions are not present in almost all transactions the appraiser should deduct for them. And consequently, one would not adjust for seller concessions when they are extremely prevalent as they are the norm. Fannie Mae's thinking is that if the subject was sold, it would also have seller concessions essentially equalizing the fact they were not calculated for in the original valuation. But they do mean *virtually all transactions*, so unless this is not the case seller concessions should be deducted for.

There are some interesting personnel appraiser interpretations of how seller concessions should be adjusted for. An instance is to deduct seller concession from the subject's sales price to form an opinion of value. Sales price $220,000 with $2,000 in seller concessions equals a value of $218,000. Also seen and another quirky practice is deducting the subject's seller concessions from each comparables sales price thus decreasing the adjusted value of each comparable by the subject's seller concession. Neither makes any sense.

Parking

This error could come from a variety of directions, but most likely from the lack of consideration given to the availability of "on street" parking. The availability of "on street" parking dictates the value of private parking. As the availability of street parking diminishes when population density increases, the value of private parking increases, yet it is common to see an appraiser make no distinction. If a homeowner feels parking has been undervalued, remember that data on the value of parking is one of the easiest to obtain, especially in urban areas. Find that data and use it as part of a rebuttal.

Second Kitchens

Second kitchens are a difficult subject. They are always a useful item for the homeowner but pose problems for underwriters as there could be legal issues. As the appraiser, is left to handle the bulk of the problem, a homeowner might want to know the answers to common questions. Just how much of a problem this is depends on the Lender. In the event there is one, the answers to these typical questions could used to justify the second kitchen. It is likely the appraiser will not consider them immediately relevant, but the chances are these questions will come up at some stage.

1) Does the second kitchen conform to building codes and allowed under the subject's current zoning? If the second kitchen is legal and frequently so, then all the better, with the appraiser simply stating that in the report. In the case of illegal kitchens the appraiser has to demonstrate they are typical for the neighborhood, and thus remain marketable, certainly for the two GSE's. This, however, can be hard to establish. There are also sections of market that will reject loans with illegal kitchens even if their commonality can be established. The whole issue is sensitive, and if in doubt check. Most Lenders, in today's market, ask homeowners to remove the gas line and stove from illegal kitchens before financing can be completed.

2) Does the second kitchen form part of an illegal rentable unit? If so the kitchen's utility and stove must be removed, but even then a wise Lender would retract. If a fire started in the rented unit would the insurance pay? Probably not, it was rented illegally.

3) Does the second kitchen form part of an accessory unit or in law unit? This is a common and permitted use for a second kitchen. Typically occupancy is permitted to family members only. If this is the case most Lenders ask for sales with in-law suites to be included in the report. There can be value is this amenity and certainly a market exist in more densely populated areas, so the appraiser should make an extended search, in time, not necessarily location.

Usually the appraiser is going to need to provide data on properties with a second kitchen as the Lender needs to establish their marketability. This data should be included as secondary data. This is, however, frequently absurd, since in certain urban and many noted suburban neighborhoods second kitchens are essential for cultural and/or ethnic reasons which lends to the sensitivity of the issue. All too often the second kitchen increases marketability. The appraiser will struggle, however, in suburban and rural areas to find sales with second kitchens. An appraiser should never let the value of a sale with a second kitchen dictate the end value, especially if that sale is not particularly comparable to begin with. Appraisers sometime describe second kitchens as "an over improvement", in other words they are not recognized by the market. Certainly in the case of finished basement that is meant for recreation this is the case, but considering their functionality and commonality in previously mentioned areas, it is hard to believe.

Comparable Photographs

Check #10. There are a few appraisers who do not drive by comparables as a part of the appraisal process. Look at the comparable photographs in the addenda and see if they are original. In the fine print of every report, there is a statement that all comparable sales are driven by and let's hope that is the case. Refer to the location map and see if any of the sales are near busy roads. Then use online aerial maps to see if any of the sales value might be affected by a State Route, a factory or negative commercial influences. If so, are these inferior locations reflected in the sales grid? If not, this is a strong indication that the comparable sales were not driven by.

Appraisers sometimes claim that comparables photos are from online sources better represent the subject at the time of sale. This opinion is not widely held, since online photos are often taken three to four months prior to the actual closing of that property, when allowing for average marketing time and the time it takes to process the loan after contract. If, however, the appraiser's opinion is that the online photographs better represent the subject at time of sale, then both online photos and the drive by photos should be included in the report. Correct appraisal practice states that all comparable sales should be driven by, no exceptions.

Analyzing Markets - What is a neighborhood?

The word *neighborhood* has different meanings, as it is accepted for the definition to vary according to academic discipline. For an appraiser the essence is:

"A neighborhood tends to be any separately identifiable, cohesive area with some community interest shared by its occupants."

Appraisers do, however, have different ideas of what a neighborhood is, and this also varies across the industry and in different parts of the country. To complicate matters the word is frequently used out of context by appraisers, Lenders and GSE's alike. For example the "neighborhood" is referenced, and the sentence should say "market area" and sometimes the word does not even apply. This creates confusion for the reader.

Breaking it down, a neighborhood is also an area which shares similar land values within a defined or recognized area. The appraiser is required to describe the neighborhood and its boundaries using co-ordinates. The value to the reader of the boundaries varies from inconsequential in rural areas, important in suburban areas to imperative in urban areas. Essentially as density increases so does the significance of location and therefore the value of a well defined neighborhood. Comparables from outside the subject's neighborhood in urban areas should have a location adjustment or a viable argument stating why none was included.

Some appraisers call a single subdivision or development a neighborhood. Unless either of these unless they are very large, this is a mistake. A school, a church and some shops are typical examples of what is needed to create a neighborhood and are typically not present when only a single subdivision or development is used. Within a neighborhood there is some tolerance for the variations in land values. In fringe areas, specifically rural or where rural borders suburban, there may be no neighborhood but just a market area comprising of competing areas.

Competing Neighborhoods, Market Area and Competing Markets

A competing neighborhood exists within the same market area as the subject. The same buyer who would consider the subject would also consider a house in a competing neighborhood. A competing neighborhood does not have to be contiguous with the subject's neighborhood, but most likely is within the same school system. The appraiser can select sales from a competing neighborhood when data is insufficient in the subject's neighborhood.

Market Area is a geographical area that comprises of a number of neighborhoods that are all affected by the same economic influences. Typical influences would be access to expressways, public transportation, employment and recreation. If data is limited in a neighborhood then the valuation is based off similar properties in the market area. The market area is also used to base market value trends.

A Competing market is a completely separate market area where a buyer would also consider buying a home, having access to similar amenities to the subject's market area. It is typical to see this term used in rural appraisals, possibly suburban, and never in urban ones. Using sales from a competing market for an appraisal in the average suburban and urban neighborhood would suggest the subject is atypical. Even then a sale's search of the prior 24 months would be preferred. A competing market is a suitable place to select sales if none are available in the subject's market area. The inclusion of data from a competing market area can be used to support opinions of market trends for an appraisal in a rural area.

The appraisers approach to neighborhoods and markets should be flexible and depend on the overall density of the area and land values. Decisions on which criteria to use would vary between urban, suburban and rural markets. In the neighborhood section of all forms the appraisers notes the build -up rate of and the present land use. Appraisers take this section too light heartedly as this information is about density and geography and sets expectations of how far sales may be located. Inconsistencies frequently exist in this section. For example if the build-up rate is between 25%-75% then the present land use should note a least a 25% other land use.

To analyze market trends some basic definitions are needed.

Market stabilization

Market stabilization is when the number of foreclosures (REO's) decline in a given market area, resulting in the median sale price to increase. Analysis of the sales however, shows the market is not actually increasing as there is no noticeable appreciation in values for standard sales. Market stabilization includes both a decrease in closed REO sales and a decrease in foreclosed properties coming to coming to market.

Increasing Markets

An increasing market starts when a number of indicators turn positive. Most importantly, a definable increase in the demand for standard sales, increasing list prices and a decline in both inventory and marketing times would be present in the data analysis. Increases below a few percent are normally not considered an increasing market. Consecutive periods of data would have to show a definable trend.

The term *markets are trending positive* is the expression of the day. This means the market is stable but there is currently insufficient evidence to say market is increasing. There may only be some improving trends, for instance shorter marketing times, a drop in inventory, a slight increase in listing prices with no notable increases in sales prices, typically below an annual rate of 5%. *Markets are trending positive* is an apt statement.

Declining Markets

Declining markets are also identified by several factors. An over-supply of property, increasing marketing times, declines in list prices, increase in REO activity, lower than expected sales price and a decline in median values are all indicators of a declining market. No single indicator is going to denote a declining market. Several of these factors would have to exist for the market to be in decline and not necessarily only a decline in median sales price.

When determining declining markets in urban areas usually researching data over one year is sufficient, while in rural areas research over a period of several years would be necessary. That said appraisers in rural areas rarely report declining market conditions in their appraisals. To see an increasing market reported in a rural appraisal is equally as rare.

Seasonal Markets

Seasonal markets exist in most Northern parts of country and in mountainous areas. Most other markets have a flurry of spring time sales, while those with hard winters do all their business in the summer months. Therefore to establish market trends analyzing markets season over season is preferred. For an appraiser this may mean including dated sales in an appraisal from the previous selling season, as better indicators of value rather than a more recent, less similar sale.

Check # 11. Borrower's living in areas where the real estate market also freezes should check the appraiser has included the most applicable sales, either from this season or the last. Lender guidelines of including recent sales may get in the way of real estate valuations in seasonal markets.

The Market Conditions Report

The market condition report (MCR) became a requirement in 2007 and is included in every residential appraisal. During the recession with property values turning south, Fannie Mae decided to create a form where the appraiser could accurately reconcile data used to analyze markets, in an easily displayable manner. But that is not what occurred, and instead the MCR has been one continuous controversy since its inception. The form has complicated the reporting of market conditions and not simplified them. Problems arise with oblique specific directions from Fannie Mae, who initially instructed appraisers to base market trends sales from the "neighborhood" using "comparables". As indicated such verbiage could mean a variety of things to various appraisers. Both of these words are emotive. Today the form gives the appraiser some leeway and the verbiage reads:

Sales and listings must be properties determined by applying the criteria that would be used by a prospective buyer for the subject property.

Most appraisers however, complete the form in the original way Fannie Mae instructed, and base trends just using comparables from the neighborhood. This leaves very little data to analyze.

The absurdity of this form is underlined by so many appraisers who complete the MCR in the manner they believe to be in accordance with Fannie Mae guidelines, and then complete their own analysis of market trends in the written addenda. Fortunately some appraisers complete the MCR in a manner that makes sense by including all applicable data.

A typical grid in the market conditions report looks something like this.

Inventory Analysis	Prior 7-12 Months	Prior 4-6 Months	Current - 3 Months	Overall Trend		
Total # of camparable Sales (Settled)	4	2	1	☐ Increasing	☒ Stable	☐ Declining
Absorption Rate (Total Sales/Months)	0.33	0.66	0.33	☐ Increasing	☒ Stable	☐ Declining
Total # of camparable Active Listings			13	☐ Increasing	☒ Stable	☐ Declining
Months of Housing Supply (Total Listings/Ab. Rate)			3.25	☐ Increasing	☒ Stable	☐ Declining
Median sales & List Price, DOM, Sale/List %	Prior 7-12 Months	Prior 4-6 Months	Current - 3 Months	Overall Trend		
Median comparable Sales Price	292,900	314,560	282,300	☐ Increasing	☒ Stable	☐ Declining
Median Comparable Sales Days on Market	94	72	67	☐ Increasing	☐ Stable	☒ Declining
Median Comparable List Price			304,900	☐ Increasing	☒ Stable	☐ Declining
Median Comparable Listing Days on Market			84	☐ Increasing	☒ Stable	☐ Declining
Median Sales Price as % of List Price	98%	93%	97%	☐ Increasing	☒ Stable	☐ Declining
Seller-(developer, builder, etc.) paid financial assistance prevalent? ☐ Yes ☒ No				☐ Increasing	☒ Stable	☐ Declining

The above data gives no real understanding of market conditions and how Fannie Mae can be happy is not readily understandable. This small data sample is statistically inadequate to establish market trends. Fannie Mae clearly asks for sufficient support in its underwriting guidelines yet is appears to be happy to accept the MCR in this manner and with no other support.

Below is an example of a MCR filled out using a database sufficient to assess value trends.

Inventory Analysis	Prior 7-12 Months	Prior 4-6 Months	Current - 3 Months	Overall Trend		
Total # of camparable Sales (Settled)	22	17	12	☐ Increasing	☒ Stable	☐ Declining
Absorption Rate (Total Sales/Months)	3.66	5.66	4	☐ Increasing	☒ Stable	☐ Declining
Total # of camparable Active Listings			13	☐ Increasing	☒ Stable	☐ Declining
Months of Housing Supply (Total Listings/Ab. Rate)			3.25	☐ Increasing	☒ Stable	☐ Declining
Median sales & List Price, DOM, Sale/List %	Prior 7-12 Months	Prior 4-6 Months	Current - 3 Months	Overall Trend		
Median comparable Sales Price	282,900	302,600	292,450	☐ Increasing	☒ Stable	☐ Declining
Median Comparable Sales Days on Market	121	89	99	☐ Increasing	☐ Stable	☒ Declining
Median Comparable List Price			304,900	☐ Increasing	☒ Stable	☐ Declining
Median Comparable Listing Days on Market			84	☐ Increasing	☒ Stable	☐ Declining
Median Sales Price as % of List Price	95%	93%	96%	☐ Increasing	☒ Stable	☐ Declining
Seller-(developer, builder, etc.) paid financial assistance prevalent? ☐ Yes ☒ No				☐ Increasing	☒ Stable	☐ Declining

Compare the conclusions from these two reports even though they are for the same property. They differ drastically from an information standpoint. A signal to the ineffectiveness of this form is the shaded areas. These fields were put in the form and then not required, as few could complete them, and never removed.

In suburban areas the appraiser should be able to complete the MCR so the reader has an idea of market trends. Sales with similar economic forces are applicable, which may mean a cluster of neighborhoods with comparable employment opportunities and transportation. This would also be the case for urban areas using sales from a well defined neighborhood. In rural areas in might not be possible to establish market within a twelve month period.

Other factors that are typically taken into for would be water and view. Waterfront property or those with desirable views typically react differently to properties with a neutral view. Foreclosures should be included in the analysis.

When preparing a MCR many appraisers pair down data and this is a good idea depending on the number of sales. In active markets a search based on age and utility is appropriate. Most appraisers however, also include property type as a criteria. In this case the appraiser is saying that a property type has a particular buyer and their reaction is sufficient to base a market trend from. This idea defies the definition of "market", in that many parties are needed for a market to exist. Property type is just preference and does not define a buyer. This is meant to be the "analysis of market trends" and not a "snap shot" of how a particular property type is performing. Basing trends on property age and utility would group buyers of similar economic standing, and it is how they react <u>as a whole</u> is what we need to know.

Real estate values move in tiers and in most markets there is just three. It sounds simple but there isn't really more than the lower, middle and upper end of the housing range. Each of these market segments would react at different times in either times of prosperity or decline, but their overall trends would follow each other, just too different degrees.

The Neighborhood Analysis Section

The neighborhood section appears at the very top of page two of the single family form and on page three of the condominium and multi-family forms. It is a small and well thought out section of the report and fits in perfectly before the presentation of the comparable sales. It gives the reader a good idea of the number of similar houses currently for sale and how many closed in the last twelve months.

The neighborhood section looks something like this.

> There are 5 comparable properties offered for sale in the subject neighborhood ranging in price from $239,500 to $274,000
>
> There are 8 comparable sales in the subject neighborhood within the past twelve months ranging in sales price from $232,000 to $269,000.

This section asks for the possible value ranges within the neighborhood. In this case there is no doubt what is required; the number of truly comparable sales and active listings. This is the total number of all sales and listings that the appraiser considered. These are then paired down to those sales included in the sales grid.

The sales prices of comparables presented in the grid should be within the range of data in the neighborhood section.

So what if there is no neighborhood? It doesn't matter, as the data would be from the same geographic region the appraiser searched for comparable sales to begin with. If the appraiser uses indicators of value from a market area then the range would be for those sales and listings.

At one point, someone, one assumes at Fannie Mae thought the data in the MCR report should correlate to the neighborhood analysis. The neighborhood analysis would be consistent if the MCR is also based on "comparables" from the "neighborhood" as in Fannie Mae original instructions. The neighborhood section is asking for directly similar properties in the neighborhood and that is all. The MCR establishes market trends and therefore these two sections are asking for two very different things, having no reason to correlate. Despite this some Lenders still ask for the two sections to be consistent. Most appraisers fully realize the difference between the neighborhood section and the MCR.

It is possible to make mistakes when completing the neighborhood section and here is one completed incorrectly.

> There are 5 comparable properties offered for sale in the subject neighborhood ranging in price from $235,000 to $275,000
>
> There are 8 comparable sales in the subject neighborhood within the past twelve months ranging in sales price from $235,000 to $275,000.

In this dataset the ranges for both closed and active are the same. The chances of the closed sale range being the same for active listings is slim and not seen when analyzing neighborhoods. This opinion is not logical.

The dataset in the neighborhood analysis should be less that the data presented in the MCR.

Comparables and Sale Selection

The sales selection seems to be a controversial point and always remains under scrutiny. In most cases there is usually good reason why those sales were used. Nonetheless the reader should have the opportunity to understand the process and have an idea of how to identify possible errors. For the purpose of this discussion the word *sale* is taken to mean the selected sale, be it directly comparable or otherwise.

Does a poor selection of sales make for a poor appraisal? Yes, it happens all the time. The appraiser, however, may not be entirely at fault being only able to consider those homes sales that are available. If the appraiser is at fault, the error may lie in poor analysis of data and using an inadequate time period to search for sales.

An actual, but admittedly extreme example is a custom home on the only lake in a suburban area. Being the only lake, property is highly sought after with no viable sales in the last twelve months. Sales choices were a "tear down" with a similar location and when combined with non lake front sales resulted in a value of $430,000. A previous appraisal however, less than eighteen months previously valued the property at $730,000, since there was one viable sale, on the lake for comparison. So what is the more probable valuation? There is nothing preventing the second appraiser using the dated sale as a basis of valuation, if accounting for subsequent market conditions. The conclusion would have to be additionally supported but in this instance the second appraisal at $430,000 appears an under valuation.

Check #12. Before refinancing should a homeowner check if there is adequate sales data to support the estimate of value? Yes, if the subject is atypical, if there is any atypical feature, or if the neighborhood is very stable with a low turnover. It is always better to know beforehand if valuation is going to be an issue.

Most reports summarize the sales selection with a phrase similar to "the selected sales are the best available". When adequate data pools exist, for example in urban and suburban areas, how does a borrower know if this statement is true? We don't since the selection of comparable sales is subjective and entirely the appraiser's opinion. There are some recognizable accepted standards, however which are useful, especially in case of dispute. These are basic standards but specific markets may have greater or less protocols for certain property types. No one can directly influence the appraiser in sales selection; neither the homeowner, loan officer/Lender, AMC nor a reviewer.

1) The appraiser's comparable selection has to make sense. The sales selection will be based on appraisal theory to include sales similar, inferior and superior to the subject property. The superior sales will be adjusted negatively while the inferior sales will be adjusted positively. This idea is known as *bracketing* and appears commonly in appraisal theory and is referenced throughout the text in difference contexts. As the name suggests the inferior and superior sales bracket the subject property. Also see over-bracketing.

2) If two comparables are similar then the appraiser should include the sale that is most proximate to the subject property or both. In the event of dispute, the sale more locationally similar will be considered superior. A wise appraiser would at least refer to the second sale differentiating their locations as part of the comments on the sales comparison approach.

3) There are various types of sales; for example, standard arms length, estate or foreclosure (REO). By all technical standards sales should be the same type, or at least the differing type of sale should be accounted. In the grid the type of sale is positioned towards the top of the sales grid which signifies its relevance in the sales selection.

Check #13. Appraisal reports tend to be blemished with un-reconciled REO sales. Therefore if the subject's transaction is arms length, is the use of a REO sale appropriate? Check that the use of any REO sales is reasoned and justified. Also check the Market Conditions Report, there is a question that asks, "Are foreclosures sales (REO sales) a factor in the market. If the answer is "No" then foreclosures should not be in the sales analysis.

4) On the first page of all appraisal forms, the appraiser states the current overall opinion of market conditions under "one unit housing trends" in the small grid just after the contract section. If the opinion is stable then all sales in the last twelve months should be considered. Appraisers discount sales because of their closing date exceeding six months, stating that it is a Fannie Mae guideline only to use sales within six months. This is incorrect as Fannie Mae only *prefers* sales in last six months. They do not want an appraiser to deter from the subject's true value by excluding more relevant data due to the sale

date. This or no other Lender guideline should detract from the subject's valuation. That said no underwriter wants to see three sales exceeding six months. Even though, as noted in seasonal markets this may be unavoidable. Underwriters can and should ask for current pending sales to show the market between 6-12 months is consistent with the current market, in cases when dated sales are used.

Homeowners get frustrated when they present sales that closed during the 6-12 month period to the appraiser, which are then rejected because of their sale date and it happens frequently.

Check #14. Has the appraiser only used sales in the last six months? If so, research which sales occurred in the six to twelve month period prior to the effective date of the appraisal. Would these sales be more relevant?

Check #15. It is worth knowing specific Lender appraisal guidelines, which exceed "Fannie Mae", especially in relation to the time and proximity of possible comparable sales. There are several investors who have their own rules in terms of appraisal guidelines. Are these restrictive and if so, would they impede a credible valuation? This is worth knowing before signing, anything.

Note 1: In either increasing or declining markets, recent sales are preferable as they signify current market activity.

Note 2: Searching for sales data can leave inadequate results. Therefore, there are no comparables rather *indicators* of value. Appraisers often use the word "comparables" in report writing when they actually mean "indicators of value".

Most appraisers employ a variety of sales searches that capture all relevant data. Nonetheless problems arise depending on the area; urban, suburban or rural. With adequate data in urban settings, data can be over refined. For example, the search is based largely on property style and the consequence is the subject's location is left behind. Clearly it would make sense to include sales both locationally similar and then more similar sales and take into account their location.

Urban homeowners complain about the lack of recognition for their location. In these cases the appraiser is frequently not familiar with the importance of the subject's location. Appraising in urban areas, even though data might seem plentiful, is meaningless without having knowledge of each individual neighborhood and sub community.

In suburban areas the sales selection may also not be perfect. Problems arise in valuations where there is a variety of housing stock in a single subdivision. These would be larger projects where the majority of the development is dedicated to mid-range housing, with some smaller homes mixed in and a few streets offered to higher end housing. Problems typically occur appraising either the smaller or executive homes as there could be no sales. The market area may have similar subdivisions and this would be a good place to find applicable sales if none are available. After all, if a buyer is in the market for either a smaller or larger home, that is what they would do. Nonetheless some appraisers compare the subject exclusively to other mid range home sales within the subject's subdivision and either adjust all sales negatively or positively depending on the circumstance to form an opinion of value. Be it in this instance or any other, this is a fundamental technical error when respecting standard valuation methods. This data does not support what the market is able to bare on the high end, and what the market will do on the low end. The opinion of value is not bracketed! In such instances the appraisal report is typically flagged either by quality control or underwriting. There is the exception of the opinion of value being marginally (1-3%) above the unadjusted range (closed sales range) which is acceptable if reasoned.

When searching for comparables, criteria are set starting with location and then physical characteristics. The criteria may include pretty much anything but not a range of values. Some appraisers do this, perhaps to save time, believing they have adequate market knowledge to put any home within a range of values. Stating that similar property sells between, $200,000 to $300,000 is taking a few things for granted and here is why.

1) Real estate markets work in tiers of values. A value tier is what the appraiser is estimating when choosing a value range to search in. These tiers are constantly changing however, and cannot be fully captured when an assumption is made. Markets are volatile and to assume the tier has remained static is incorrect.

2) Similar searches are liable to exclude lower selling properties such as foreclosures and tear-down sales. The latter could be used to estimate land value. In addition the appraiser needs to be aware of the total number of foreclosures in the subject's neighborhood and surrounding area. The results are included in the market conditions report (MCR).

3) These searches also exclude new construction and any higher end homes that might or might not be present in the market. New construction is an indication of revitalization. While if competitively priced new homes continue to languish on the market, this might be sign of a weak market.

4) Searching for comparables within a value range will cut out sales data that could be used for calculating adjustments specifically land.

5) A fundamental part of the appraiser's job is to analyze data. Considering the simple series of data appraisers encounter, selecting value ranges to analyze is only appropriate if all other value ranges are analyzed. Appraisers have a tendency to stray from statistical theory.

As said sales searches can consist of pretty much anything. There is an extended form of "bracketing" that not only includes superior and inferior properties but also used to refer to sales that have a similar feature to the subject. Appraisers sometimes state, "Comparable 3 was included to bracket the subject's two acre lot". In other words comp 3 has three acres while comps 1 and 2 had only one acre. Therefore the lot size has been bracketed by comp 3. This is normal appraisal practice but what happens if the appraiser continues to do this through-out the sales section. Sale 1 included as it has a finished basement, sale 2 as it has in ground pool and sale 4 to bracket which if the subject is older might not be necessary. This concept is known as over- bracketing and is a problem in many sale selections. The over bracketing of a property can lead to a mis-valuation.

Check #16. Read through the verbiage and look for any references that might indicate a problem in respect to the sales search. Many appraisers describe their search criteria in the appraisal report. Valid questions to ask are: *Would the search equal the one made by a home buyer?* and *What geographic area did the appraiser use to search for sales?*

How is an Adjustment Calculated?

Appraisers adjust for differences between the subject and comparable sales to reduce their differences. The comparable sale prices after adjustment creates an adjusted range in values of the closed sales, giving a basis for valuation. The correct method of calculating an adjustment depends on the type, for example a lot size adjustment is calculated in a different manner than a condition adjustment. To create an adjustment some kind of calculation is typically completed for that feature and combined with the appraiser's market knowledge. For some adjustments it's mostly calculation while others are based more on the appraiser opinion. When all factors are combined adjusting for comparable sales is the most subjective part of the appraisal process.

There are some property aspects that are not adjusted for. There are general industry standards and most appraisers adhere to them. On the odd occasion it's a mistake to adhere to the standard. Typically speaking these are things the appraiser is unable to extract, being too small an adjustment objectively or otherwise.

1) Variances in gross living area of less than 100 sq. ft. After this threshold the total difference in square footage is adjusted for. This practice, however in some cases is a mistake. In the example of high density living this threshold is too high. Condominiums typically react more readily to square footage, yet appraisers have a tendency to treat them equally to residential properties in terms of GLA adjustment criteria.

2) Total room count: Typically appraisers do not adjust for the total number of rooms, preferring to include this variance in the adjustments for gross living area. There are exceptions, see Functional Utility.

3) Whether the appraiser adjusts for lot size depends on the total land value and not necessarily the lot size. Land value lies in its location and utility.

a) In rural settings lot size adjustments are usually not applicable within one or two acres; even then there could be reasons why larger variance are not accounted.

b) Suburban areas are more sensitive to land value, with the appraiser usually adjusting on the lots utility and then size. From observation the median variance for suburban appraisers to adjust for lot size is approximately 20%.

c) Lot size variances in urban areas of high land value, usually dictate an adjustment and at least an explanation if none are included. It is normal to adjust on a front foot basis in medium to high density urban areas as this creates utility and therefore value. "Front Foot" is the number of feet the property faces the street.

d) Comparables sales occasionally offer noticeably varying lot sizes and adjustments appear inconsistent. In these cases the appraiser is adjusting for total land value as there is a variance in each sale's location. Perhaps the sales are from competing neighborhoods. Some kind of explanation should be offered.

e) Lot size adjustments might not be applied to a subdivision lot versus a nearby small acreage parcel. The value of the smaller lot is increased with public sewer, water, curbs, gutters and streetlights while the larger lot does not share these features thus creating similar values. This situation may exist when suburbia starts to encroach into less densely populated areas.

4) Detached versus attached garages. Most homeowners believe an attached garage does add value especially in colder climates but in many cases this is not an extractable adjustment. Garages are counted per stall and the appraiser is not able to account for anything less. A two garage has a similar value to a two and a half car garage.

5) Small Amenities. The typical small garden shed does not contribute a value that is readily identifiable even if does have a foundation.

A term called "pairing sales" is the most common method of calculating an adjustment. The appraiser is taught that a paired sale is taking two identical properties with one varying feature and the difference in the value is the adjustment for that feature. In reality there is limited data to get any paired sales to be that precise, especially with factors like terms of sale and property condition to consider. Therefore this idea does have limitations. The data is also just one "pair of sales" and therefore only one indicator of what the adjustment should be which is not positive in some eyes. Nonetheless it is accepted appraiser practice to analyze adjustments for view, land, differing number of bedrooms and garages in this manner. Pairing sales, on single sets of data at least, is not an appropriate approach for smaller items like decks, patios, porches or fireplaces.

In a complex market the appraiser employs applied knowledge to the simple theory of "paired sales". The methodology would depend on the sought adjustment. Frequently the appraiser will try and exclude as many variables in the equation as possible. See GLA adjustments below.

Land Adjustments

Consider receiving an appraisal with a property value of $644,000 and a land value of $225,000. The lot is 19,000 sq. ft and most of the comparables are on 10,000 sq. ft. There are no land/site adjustments and no comments included. The only way this could make sense, remembering the lots are in the same neighborhood, is if 10,000 sq. ft lots sold for the same price as those twice their size. This is effectively what the appraiser is saying by stating there is no market reaction to lot size. But this is unlikely as by dividing the land value by the total property value leaves land value at 35%. Receiving an appraisal with no lot size adjustment, when by all account one is due is a common example homeowner's face. The only way to disprove the lack of land adjustment is via finding data on land values either from vacant or improved sites.

What significance, if any, does the assessed land value have and can an appraiser use this data to base lot adjustments from? Considering the assessor's office uses an assessed value and an appraiser uses market value then the consensus is "No". The assessor does mass valuations and does not always take into account; market conditions, external inadequacies, buyer preferences together with utility and condition of the lot either wooded or level, all of which play a role. Some assessors are more finite than others. There are appraisers who use assessed land values in their reports for the subject's land value which is not that informative. Using assed land values to adjust for varying lot sizes is very questionable. The appraiser's justification that land sales are scarce, and the assessor's data is consistent is understandable but not correct. Technically an appraiser uses raw market data to base lot size adjustments from. There are a few methods available if there are recent vacant land sales or not.

a) Paired sales of improved sites, so if two houses are similar the difference is the amount the additional land is contributing to value.

b) Via calculating price per square foot of unimproved buildable lots based on land sales over a period of 24 months. So with two equalized land sales at $24 and $26 per square foot for 10,000 sq ft and 12000 sq. ft lots respectively, would suggest a $2 market reaction for the additional land. As if comparable's 2 lot is 3,000 sq ft larger this indicates an adjustment of $6,000 is due.

c) It helps to know building costs and depreciation as an option to calculate how much value the land contributed to each sale in the report. That can be compared to the subject's land value and an adjustment extracted thereafter. This calculation is not easy, as depreciation is difficult to measure, but if the subject is new or within five even ten years of construction this can work well.

d) Water front homes are also adjusted on a front foot basis as the actual size of the land may not be as important as the lot's access to water. Similar to areas of high land values, the appraiser takes into account utility and adjusts on a front footage basis.

Factors that create value on water vary between lake, channel, canal and ocean. Listed below are some of the main examples but there are many varying on region and location.

Lake. Common factors that create value on lakes are; view, front footage, beach, water depth, open water, swimming and other recreational uses.

Channel. Typically worth less than lake front homes but view and water depth are important along with front footage.

Canal. The value in canals depends on access to open water and front footage. A canal would have adequate water depth.

Ocean. Ocean views are compared similarly to large lake views like those seen around the Great Lakes. Factors assessed are view, water front footage, beach type, pebble or sandy, privacy and prevailing winds and surf.

Check #17. The subject's land value is in the cost approach to value. This section is on page 3 of the single family form, on page 4 of the 2-4 unit form and would not be applicable for a condominium. Check the estimate of land to total property value ratio. Would the ratio incur land adjustments? Does the subject have a superior view that is not adjusted for?

Condition Adjustments

Homeowners are frequently upset over condition adjustments in a report believing their home improvements bring value. Concerns cover an array of aspects but usually mention the kitchen. As this is the case let's use the kitchen as an example and try and estimate the maximum additional value a new or newer kitchen will bring. This value will always be discounted by the market and a part of the appraiser's overall condition adjustment.

To calculate the <u>maximum</u> value a kitchen can contribute consider the average cost to replace a kitchen in a home similar to yours and apply it as a base figure. For example the replacement cost of a new kitchen is $12,000 excluding appliances and will survive 15 years of wear and tear.

If the subject's recently "remodeled" kitchen is 3 years old and also expected to last for 15 years, then this kitchen has lost 20% of its value leaving 80% of $12,000, worth $9,600.

The comparable with an older kitchen, which the real estate agent states, is 9 years old has 6 years left before it needs replacing. Therefore its worth 6/15 years, or 40% of $12,000 or $4,800.

This means the difference in value between the two kitchens is $9,600-$4800=$4,800 and this is the maximum that could be adjusted for. $4,800 is already a long way off the subject's depreciated value of $12,000. The appraiser will use judgment thereafter, reducing the $4,800 via estimating the market reaction to determine the actual adjustment. If modernized kitchens are typical for this market, or at least expected by a buyer, only a fraction would be applied.

Condition adjustments seen in reports are a lump sum. Sometimes additional condition adjustments, for kitchen and bathroom modernization are included on the last three lines of the sales grid.

Most likely the condition adjustment within the average report is a best guess estimate. Appraisal practice does ask for condition adjustments to be explained, as any adjustment above the base-line (basement line) should be. These explanations refer to what was inferior or superior in the comparables. An incorrect description for a condition adjustment would explain the differences in the subject. This is not necessary as the subject condition is already a known fact. It is the differences in the comparables when compared to the subject that is important. If the condition adjustment is questioned it's an inadequate explanation to state the adjustments was based off interior photography of each comparable.

Some estate real agents photo-shop the interior photographs, leaving the appraiser to make judgment errors in respect to condition.

Gross Living Area

For Lenders and homeowner GLA adjustments need the most explanation. Despite this a brief explanation of how the GLA adjustment is calculated is rarely included. Nonetheless it's interesting to see if the GLA adjustment is reasonable.

Gross living area is the principal composition of the house. Therefore to isolate the value of just the home on price per square foot basis, the value of all exterior factors (the variables) are removed starting with the largest. Calculating the value of the land, then garage, and any amenities including out-buildings leaves the value of the house itself. These data-sets are simplified if the appraiser was able to use sales similar in quality of construction and below grade finishes.

The chart shows the maximum amount the appraiser could contribute to GLA.

	COMP 1	COMP 2	COMP 3	Subject
PRICE	$292,300	$327,400	$264,500	$295,000
LAND VAL	-$80,000	-$95,000	-$70,000	-70000
GARAGE	-$12,000	-$17,000	-$12,000	-12000
Outbuildings				
Amenities	-$2,000	-$4,000	-$2,000	-$2000
Quality/Con'tion	$0	$0	+8000	
NET TO GLA	$198,300	$211,400	$188,500	$211,000
GLA	2329	2774	2170	2424
GLA /Sq ft.	$85	$76	$86	$87

Note quality of construction and condition adjustments are positive, in this case. Values are equalized and comp 3 is the variance.

Again the appraiser will use a lower number than those stated in the above grid to adjust for GLA. Most GLA adjustments range in the 25%-35% of total price per square foot, located on the line the below the sales price, in the sales comparison approach section. Appraisers tend be static in their approach to GLA adjustments and insufficiently account for external factors. In the case of land value GLA adjustments per square foot are lowered for a high land value and conversely higher for lower land values.

Check #18. GLA adjustments are normally completed on a consistent price per square foot basis. Check the $ per square foot is consistent. Technically speaking the price per square foot does not have to be consistent but usually is for residential property. If not the reader is owed a viable explanation.

When adjusting for GLA, there can be errors or indications of them.

a) The appraiser can get tangled in a direct paired sale and use that a basis for analysis without sufficiently considering the variables.

b) To read a comment, "A flat $X per square foot is adjusted for all homes in this market" or "It is common practice to $X per square foot". Both do not bode well.

c) GLA adjustments are higher in condominiums than in single family homes as there is no land, therefore the value of gross living area increases. Lack of parking, amenities and view, which are the other significant factors when appraising a condominium, would also increase the relevance of GLA. Appraisers have a tendency to forget this.

Check # 19. Calculate the GLA adjustment per square foot and compare to total price per square of foot for each sales. This is found under the sales price in the grid. If the subject is a condominium does this number seem low?

<u>Basements</u>

Basements can be adjusted up to three times, firstly, for their access, then overall square footage and finally for how the basement is finished. The basement area is never included in gross living area, it is a separate entity and the adjustments process shows that. The adjustments applied to basements are generally low and typically less than their actual contributory value. Most appraisers apply basement adjustments on a subjective basis. Certainly in some circumstances, rural areas, for example, it is understandable but in more densely populated areas where basements are common, there is no reason why these adjustments could not be objectively supported. An adjustment for a property with a basement versus without and finished versus unfinished can be supportable in most suburban and urban areas. This is assuming they are typical to the market and in many parts of the country they are not. Basement utility adjustments, the specific finishes, are hard to support no matter the location. Adjustments for number of rooms, bars, baths, sauna, spas, and standard of finishes along are going to be subjective. The variances for finished areas sometimes appear in the overall adjustment for basement square footage.

Energy Efficient Items

An effort is being made to recognize "green" and energy efficient items (EEIs), but there are problems. Most notably is the variety of EEI's which could be $1000 in rain barrels, to $50,000 in thermo dynamic heating. Rain barrels would only increase marketability and shave a little off the water bill and have no effect on value, while the heating system would save the homeowner a significant expense for an indefinite period. Data is usually limited to base EEI's adjustments from. Some EEI's might be common in a neighborhood but owners who install them, usually do so with the intention of staying and reaping the rewards. This leaves few if any "paired sales" to base an adjustment from. There are a few ideas however.

a) For features like solar panels, builders may include them in their designs. Sales would indicate what a buyer is willing to pay for this feature compared to a house without.

b) The prior three years could be researched and for data and that adjustment translated into a percentage and then applied to the comparables. Translating the dollar figure into a percentage takes out market volatility. Using a percentage could be applied to other types of adjustments that require data from an extended period of time.

c) The appraiser can also use the income stream produced from the energy efficient items to calculate an adjustment. Most appraisers would have difficulty performing this task.

Considering these possibilities an energy efficient adjustment immediately distinguishes itself from any other adjustment as the benefit of income needs to be calculated.

Homeowners can help by finding out if builders are installing similar features, asking a real estate agent and calling the electricity company, finding out the going rate for 1000kw. Whatever the savings are compared to the average home or the *income stream*, prepare a statement showing initial cost to install, benefit on a monthly/yearly basis, including maintenance costs, and give this to the appraiser. It is harder for the appraiser to deny an adjustment if information is given.

Hopefully when the real estate market gets more adept at recognizing and applying value to energy efficient items, the report could include a section grading the house in question encompassing a variety of EEI's. Currently there is one line in the sales comparison approach grid to adjust for EEI's.

Due to their rudimentary nature smaller items like average energy efficient windows or tank-less water heaters will not attract an adjustment from the appraiser.

Check # 20. The report may well describe how and what methods the appraiser uses to adjust. This may be stock verbiage but is useful to the reader if it is up to date. Some appraisers include in the text the amount some items are adjusted for like price per square foot for GLA, lot sizes, bathrooms and garages.

How a Reconciliation Reads?

A reconciliation or summary of the appraisal report, formulates the appraiser's opinion of value within the sales adjusted range in values. Convention dictates the appraiser summarizes all the approaches to value; the sales comparison approach, the cost approach and the income approach. Not all approaches are needed to form an opinion of value. The sales comparison approach, some may call it market approach, is fundamental to valuation while the other two approaches relevance varies upon circumstance. A discussion in the report on the relevance of the cost approach would be appropriate for properties which are new or recently built. If the subject is a rented condominium, the income approach maybe an indicator especially in urban areas where a rental markets exist. If either of these two approaches are not used the reader is given a brief explanation why.

The reconciliation is an under reported section of the report, yet it is also the final chapter. The typical verbiage found in most reports rarely correlates the value within the range or discusses the relevance of market trends. This lack of reporting is largely a product of so many years of stable real estate markets.

A well worded reconciliation is especially important in times of volatile markets. The appraiser needs to clarify the sales comparison approach. Specifically, the reconciliation needs a clear opinion why the value is at the lower, middle or high end of the adjusted sales range and which comparable sales held the most weight in that determination.

Check # 21. Appraisers frequently include information applicable to the reconciliation under the comments for the sales comparison approach. It is also common for the appraiser to split sales comparison approach comments between the given area under the sales grid and add additional comments in the addenda. So if the comments on the form are limited there may be more clarification deeper in the report. Additionally comments are commonly found on page three of the single form or page four of the multi family forms, above the cost approach.

The appraiser may have an opinion of value below the sales price. In this case the reader, be it the homeowner or underwriter needs to fully understand why the subject is overpriced. Frequently appraisers believe this is not their function to compare contract price and appraised value, but an explanation remains good appraisal practice. Secondly this is the mortgage industry and there is an expectation to tell the homeowner or buyer, real estate agent if applicable, loan officer and underwriter why the contract price is not supported. The reason could be apparent but frequently isn't. An appraiser needs to have the emotional intelligence to realize why this important, just from an empathy stand-point. A homebuyer may have the opportunity to renegotiate the contract in which case this information is needed, to tell the seller why the price is too high.

One would deem the explanation fair considering the common circumstance of a borrower agreeing to a sales price after competing with other homebuyers, only to find the market value is less than contract price. This is tough, as sometimes the homebuyer loses the house to a competitor and might not do so if the appraiser articulated why the sales price was too high. If this second party is able to buy the property and if the subject will ever appraise at contract remains another question.

A typical reconciliation found in most appraisal report reads.

Most weight was placed on the sales comparison approach. The cost approach is not considered. The income approach is not considered a reliable indicator of value as most homes are owner occupied. The sales price is not supportable.

The reader does understand this is a summary report and there may be a few other comments in the comparison approach, but isn't this taking the idea of "summary" too far. A reconciliation of a summary appraisal report should comment on the range of adjusted values giving reference points to the reasoning. A reconciliation does not state why any of the comparable sales are included, as those comments are applicable in that section.

Here is an example of how reconciliation might read.

The adjusted comparable sales show a range in value of $284,500 to $315,500. The opinion of value is $305,000. With positive market conditions (see market condition report) the opinion of value would tend to the mid to higher end of the range. Comparable 4 which has the highest adjusted value was partially discounted being in walking distances to commuter transportation.

Most weight has been placed on comparables 1 # 2 for their similarity in proximity and condition. Least weight has been placed on comparable 3, an estate sale, included to show the reader a base line value. The opinion of value is additionally supported by current market activity through pending sale #5 and a recent market listing comparable #6. The subject's good marketability offering modernization was considered in the overall opinion.

The cost approach is not considered due to the subject's age and the strength, in this case, of the sales comparison approach. The income approach is similarly not relevant as only 5-10% of homes in the area are currently rented.

Then there is the possible addition.

The subject's contract price is not supported by the current market. The subject's list and contract price are above any comparables sales sold in the last 12 months and above the adjusted comparable sales range. The subject has been modernized but these improvements are expected and typical for the market and similar to comparable 2.

1732 Greengate St was not included for comparison as this sale was 24% larger than the subject in terms of GLA and competes with other executive homes. Comparables #4 and #5 are both competing active listings with adjusted values less than the contract price.

Check #22. If the appraiser states the contract price is not supportable, then that number technically should not appear in two places in the report. Firstly within the adjusted range of the sales themselves and secondly within the range of values seen in the neighborhood section at the top of page two. This is a technical rule, and if for any reason this is the case the appraiser needs to state why any adjusted sales or otherwise held less weight in the final opinion.

The sales price does hold some weight in the opinion of value or at least should. Most appraisers would balk at that statement, as to ignore the sales price is how many are trained. Nonetheless the fact that someone, assuming this is an arm's length transaction, is willing to pay the negotiated price, does count for something when considering the definition of market value. If there is a well supported range in values and the appraiser is looking for the most probable value, then the most likely value is the negotiated price. Remember a segment from the definition of value which states, *"The buyer and seller, each acting prudently, knowledgeably and assuming the price is not affected by undue stimulus"*, and that probable value is an adjusted value. So after the appraiser has established a range, the perfect adjustor is the market itself. Appraising is a form of applied economics and its underlying rules come from basic economic principles. Appraisers sometimes forget this.

Contract prices resulting from bidding wars do not conform to the definition of market value as there is undue stimulus and it's questionable if the buyer is acting prudently.

Quality of Data and How it Affects Appraisals?

Can we agree that in a perfect world we would have perfect data leading to perfect appraisals? That would be nice!

The appraiser needs two verifiable data sources to include a sale in a report. The complete listing, showing closed sales price and date is usually one, and then a second is needed. This could be public, subscription or private; the source just has to be verifiable. All information sources are cited in the sales grid on the fourth and fifth lines titled "data and verification sources".

The quality of data made available to appraisers varies from State to State, again in the County level, throughout townships and from town to town. In my State, there is a County to the North, where the appraiser is given excellent data on property characteristics, making the assignment easier to complete. While to the South there is data for part of a County and the remainder is blank.

An appraiser may choose a dozen properties for consideration, only find a fraction of the information needed to use the sale in report. When basic information; lot sizes, year built, gross living area is missing from property data sheets it makes the appraisers' job difficult. There are a number of assessors who, over the years, have made a better effort at providing accurate information while others languish, most likely from the lack of recourses. Typically speaking, the quality of data is adequate in more densely populated areas and sparse in rural areas. Access to data is fundamental to the continuance and vibrancy of real estate markets.

What happens if an appraiser selects a sale for comparison and finds there is no data? None of the choices are good. The appraiser may try some long shots, perhaps the selling estate agent has a survey or did a peer appraise that sale? More often than not the appraiser chooses an alternative sale with a data. This leaves behind a sale that would have been a good indicator of value. This affects the valuation quality.

Assessors hold property cards for each parcel of land in their area, which can be found online and/or at the assessor's office. It's worth knowing how the local assessor works and reports. The property card information shows the assessor's number for that parcel with pertinent property characteristics. The information may have mistakes and reporting methods might vary from how the appraiser will work.

For example, gross living area, GLA may be calculated (GLA) in different ways. An appraiser will likely include a finished attic in the GLA while it's common for an assessor to note it as a separate item. Then there are some assessors who report the GLA of a bi level property in a different manner to the appraiser. A bi level property usually has a lower level with a portion below grade, and the assessor may include this in GLA while the appraiser following typical reporting standards will not.

Check #23. Cross reference the gross living areas of your home with each sale using the assessor's website. Typically the online data for all sales matches that seen in the report for age, lot size and GLA. For the subject there might be variances in GLA as the appraiser measured this himself and an acceptable difference is expected.

As mentioned the appraiser also uses verified closed sales prices from listing sheets as a data-source. There are some States where the sales price of property is not publicly disclosed. These States are called "Non Disclosure States" and are Alaska, Idaho, Indiana, Kansas, Louisiana, Maine, Mississippi, Missouri, Montana, New Mexico, North Dakota, Texas, Utah, and Wyoming. The appraiser accesses sales information from subscription services. This system makes it tough for homeowners, who are in a value dispute, to independently find sales prices of possible comparables. In today's society with real estate being so much of the average person wealth this seems to create a conflict with the public needs and right for information.

In some cases there is no online assessor or multiple listing service and the appraisers make regular trips to the court house to find sales and or verify information. In these cases homeowners have to follow similar steps to verify the data within their report. When checking information remember some properties have two of even several parcels numbers.

Neither the homeowner nor the appraiser should take the assessor's information at face value. Has the appraiser translated the property's information directly? Errors do exist and most seem to originate from the two previously mentioned problems; finished attic areas and bi-levels. The appraiser may use a GLA assuming the finished attic area is included when in fact the assessor has excluded it. This would lead to a low valuation.

An appraiser should judge each attic for what it is; second or third floor, dormered, skylights or otherwise. If the space has steep inclining walls, with limited natural light, then clearly this area would contribute less per square foot than the first floor. Therefore this attic area shouldn't be included in GLA, but valued as a separate item in the sales grid. Conversely an attic showing adequate height, the result of numerous dormers, is going to contribute similarly to the first floor and should be included in GLA.

Bi-level reporting errors start when the assessor and then the appraiser include both upper and lower levels in GLA. This is acceptable, not from an appraising standpoint, but for reporting purposes, if the appraiser is consistent with the sales presentation. It helps if the subject and all comparables are the same style, i.e. bi-levels. Problems begin when the appraiser treats upper and lower levels, between the subject and comparable sales, in an inconsistent manner. This means co-mingling upper and lower levels to form GLA for some sales and not for others. The valuation results can be questionable and usually are.

In some cases assessor's records are simply outdated. In either vibrant real estate markets where new homes or additions are common, or where records do not always reflect the actual improvements, appraisers need to be astute to possible discrepancies. In many ways this is the purpose of the drive-by inspection for comparable sales, but unfortunately errors creep into appraisals reports as a direct consequence of the mis-interpretation of assessor information.

Rebuttals and Creating One

When there is a dispute between borrower and appraiser, a rebuttal is written. A rebuttal can be over any issue and not necessarily value. An appraiser, upon receiving a rebuttal from a homeowner, might want to take a minute to sit back and read the argument, checking their data and supporting arguments before making a decision on the rebuttals' validity. Valid or not the responses homeowners receive to their rebuttals are brief and frequently leave more questions.

Check#24. Look over the rebuttal response checking the appraiser's comments and especially their structure. Has the appraiser actually written or used stock verbiage and platitudes. At this stage the appraiser response is an indicator of professionalism.

Inadequate responses to rebuttals can be traced back to a few things. Perhaps, due to the commonality of a particular appraiser receiving one, but most likely the homeowner's rebuttal was poorly worded and the arguments held little weight. For example rebuttals based <u>entirely</u> on a subjective argument, like condition, will not attract the appraiser's attention. The overall approach is key, yet homeowners and real estate agents have a tendency to be emotive and loan officers can be vociferous, none of which help. Some rebuttals should not be submitted in the first place. Conversely there are portions based on valid complaints and these are of interest.

Rebuttals traditionally have a very low success rate with an estimate of less than 5%, succeeding. The success rate should be higher! The poor approach is part of the problem, but maybe coupled with a lack of humility by the appraiser to admit a mistake. In addition to these problems there is another force working against the borrower's arguments. AMC's dislike an appraiser to have a change of heart as this translates into an admission of error. The AMC has a contract with the Lender, part of it being, only to engage competent appraisers... so how does that look? Yet it's never about the mistake and always about the way it's resolved.

Despite all of this, a well thought out rebuttal can go a long way. A rebuttal takes time and energy to produce and process. The loan officer, processors at Lenders and AMC's, and of course the appraiser are all going to be involved, so make it good. You are rebutting a "legal document" so at least be formal and detailed.

After reading through the appraisal and it is decided there are errors, discrepancies, inconsistencies or possible poor comparable selection, what is the best way to rebut the appraiser's opinions?

Decide what kind of discrepancies these are. Are they something the appraiser will not adjust for anyway or is the variance a concern? (see Common Appraisal Mistakes and How is an Adjustment Calculated). Write down, on a separate piece of paper, all the things the appraiser needs to address. Start with any discrepancies going through each section starting on page one of whatever form it is. Check the primary data, the gross living area and other entries for the subject in the improvements section and make sure they are consistent with the entries in sales comparison approach and then remainder of data entries in the grid for the comparables. Adjacent to each error write down the support or data-source. Acceptable sources are assessors, townships, courthouse records, surveys, personal sketches with dimensions and calculations, and building plans with dimensions.

The opinions of real estate agents will not be considered as support for a rebuttal argument, if not supported with data. Real estate agents often refer to more favorable sections of established neighborhoods as part of the argument. So if a particular part of a neighborhood is more favorable, use data over several years to demonstrate that. Show the limited sales in the favorable section compared to the questioned sale's location, year over year to establish that a pattern of higher sales prices exists.

Real estate agents recognize certain property aspects and appraisers may not. These items serve more to demonstrate the subject's marketability which creates value, but the appraiser struggles to identify it. For example, cul-de-sac locations versus a typical residential street, mature landscapes, modernizations and a larger garage, the list goes on depending on circumstance. This is the identifiable line between real estate agents and appraisers in terms of perspective. The real estate agent needs to find market value, while the appraiser needs to support market value.

An agent is nonetheless a useful person to have in the same corner, even if the rebuttal is for a refinance. That agent will no doubt get your business at a later date if they can make a contribution. So why not call up the local real estate office and ask? They can provide data on current market conditions and their input on sales is useful. Compare the agent's sales and comments and ask, are they actually superior to what the appraiser has included and will these arguments be recognized? Write down several points why.

As stated the appraisal report in hand is a summary report, so when questions are asked in a rebuttal, the appraiser uses his complete file to answer them. Some homeowners get frustrated when they pose questions and get no reasonable answer. It can be that this information is beyond the appraiser's scope of work and therefore not in the file. This has to be accepted assuming the initial scope of work, to base valuation on, was adequate. If the question is pertinent to the valuation process it's within the scope of work.

Typically homeowner's lead their rebuttal with a question about condition. Condition is subjective and very difficult to argue. As seen in the list of arguments below it is one of the least effective. When condition adjustments appear unreasonable or not supported with any logic, the correct question to pose is, "Appraiser to provide specific analysis to support condition adjustments". Then say why you need that information, which is, there appears to be discrepancies. Be specific about the condition of all properties in question. Use the three page appendix (see Understanding an Appraisal), if necessary which defines the condition categories and point out any discrepancies there. Condition arguments are best used as supporting arguments to the general inappropriateness of a comparable and not as a main argument.

Check #25. The comparable sales in the grid may describe the same condition such as C3, but still contain an adjustment. This is acceptable but these need to explained in detail.

Go back to the list of issues formulated when reviewing the appraisal and try to place them in order of importance. A rebuttal does not have to contain each one of the following, far from it, and the following are loosely ranked in terms of how much weight each argument holds. That said, the first point would be the most important. One hopes, however, that this point is not a part of anyone's rebuttal.

1) Possible issues with unacceptable appraisers practice. See *Unacceptable appraisal practices* below

2) Variances in market conditions, supported with data.

3) Differences in physical data such as GLA, lot sizes, age between what is in the appraisal and other reliable sources that would have an effect in value. Refer to –what is not adjusted for, under *How is an adjustment calculated.*

4) Inconsistencies in the report. Possible instances of inconsistencies are mentioned throughout the text. Summarize the arguments and point out discrepancies both within the report and based on data.

5) The circumstances of the included sales. Did the appraiser include a foreclosed property and place too much weight (value) on that sale unnecessarily?

6) The location of sales. Note sales located outside the neighborhood and support possible location adjustments with data.

7) This section includes a variety of problems, see *Common Appraisal Mistakes* and *How is an Adjustment Calculated* . They include a lack of adjustments, inconsistent adjustments and across the board adjustments. Any implausible adjustments and insufficiently explained condition adjustments would be questioned.

8) Technical errors. Any technical error adds important weight to an argument. Common technical errors include.

a) If the opinion of value is outside either the sales sold price range (on the top of the grid) or the sales adjusted value range (the bottom of the grid) without reason.

b) If page 1 states that markets are increasing and the value is at the low end of the range.

c) If the opinion of value does not appear in the range shown in the neighborhood inventory analysis at the top of the sales comparison approach section.

After that start writing! Here is an example of a rebuttal including examples of typical problems homeowners face.

Start with an introduction.

> *We refer to the appraisal report, street name and number, completed by your company on the date of. We have verified the data collected by the appraiser for our property and for those sales noted in the comparable sales selection. We believe that the comparable selection when combined with the noted discrepancies has led to a valuation that is questionable when considering, for example, positive markets conditions.*

Address any issues with the opinion of markets trends/ conditions. Refer to and attach as much support as possible, remembering that one or two indicators may not signify a move in market conditions.

According to the attachment the opinion of market trends is not currently stable but has been increasing for at least two consecutive periods. In your report the data sample in the market conditions report is very small and there is no additional data within the report to support stable markets. The data samples presented in the report are deemed statistically unreliable by any reasonable mathematical or professional standard. The data we have supplied is for our neighborhood and we have included additional data on Salisbury Plains, a competing neighborhood that is contiguous to ours, together with data from the whole market area. All these show an increase above 5% for more than two consecutive periods, X% and Y%. The increase in values shows, at the very least, the opinion of value should not be at the low end of the comparable adjusted range (and then site the adjusted range).

There are two listings included in the report, both with lower market times than the cited average marketing time in the report. We understand these listings are not directly considered but are an indication of the current market. Currently listed comparables 4 and 5 are in the immediate neighborhood; of similar age and show adjusted values above the opinion of value by X% and Y%. This provides further support that the opinion of market trends is incorrect. Apart from limited data in the market condition report, what we received has no viable opinion of market trends, an inadequate reporting standard.

Check # 26. Are any of the comparable sales in areas of differing land values? Discuss any noted problems between the relationship of the subject and the comparables' location. Data would have to accompany a differing opinion of land values. When preparing data use the same set of neighborhood boundaries the appraiser uses, these are on page one of all forms.

The neighborhood boundaries include an acceptable and recognized geographic area. Comparable 2, however, is not located in the described boundaries. There is no explanation in the report to the location of comparable 2 when compared to the subject property except for a remark, "That all comparables come from the same market area". This is a concern as property values vary outside our general neighborhood. Please see attached data (over several years) showing that properties in this area consistently sell for less than in our neighborhood.

As an alternative to comparable 2, we have attached a similar sale that is within the stated neighborhood and question why a sale further away was preferred to 125 Green St, considering their overall similarity.

Check #27. Are the sale conditions of each comparable appropriate and similar arms length sales or are some sales foreclosures?

The number of foreclosures in our neighborhood is minimal yet comparable 3 is a foreclosure. This sale, despite being within close proximity to our house is not a suitable comparable due to the type of sale. Comparable 3 sold for x% below comparable 1, also a similar property and a standard sale. Foreclosure rates are less than X% and believe it is unnecessary to include a foreclosed sale, even misleading when similar standard sales are available. Your opinion of value is the same as the adjusted value (or X% from the adjusted value) to this foreclosed property. Therefore it seems you have placed most weight on this sale even though this sale, or any other is not reconciled in the report. Please refer to your MCR where it states that foreclosures are not a factor in the neighborhood.

I have made an effort to contact our new neighbor and have attached a list of deferred maintenance they found in the property at the time of purchase. None of which exist in our home which is described as well modernized. The element of unknown condition would make this sale inappropriate for use. You report has not (or inadequately) accounted for both circumstance and condition of this sale which is unreasonable considering aforementioned points and discrepancies.

Discuss disparities between the subject and comparables in age, lot size and data entry errors:

Our house is built in 1998 while comparables 2 and 3 are some 20 years older. Comparable 1 is 10 years older. It has already been stated why comparables 2 and 3 are not suitable together with sale 3 but our house is compared to older homes in all cases. Sale 1 adjusted value is X% higher than the opinion of value. Considering this is an older home than ours, with less square footage this sale would represent the lower end of the value range rather than higher. There are no comments on why age adjustments are not included. The comparable we present is more similar in age and quality of construction than all the comparables used in the report.

The land value noted in the appraisal is at 25% of value opinion or $75,000. The sales lots sizes varies by -6%, -16%, -12%, -1% and +2% respectively when compared to my lot. The corresponding adjustments to the comparables sales price are 0%, +2%, +1%, 0% and 0% respectively. As stated comparable 2 is located in an area of lower land values, which we have supplied data on. The lots sizes of comparables 2 and 3 are also significantly smaller. The utility of comparable 3 is limited being a corner lot. All these factors indicate the report is not cognizant of location and lot size/value and the adjustments included are unreasonable. Is it that an adjustment is due for a patio and not for a property aspect with significantly higher contributory value?

We have attached a list of data entry errors and would like these rectified in the report. These errors further demonstrate show the ill-prepared nature of the supplied document.

It is preferred that the appraiser takes a fresh look at market conditions and the sale at 125 Green St. Data also shows the neighborhood of Salisbury Plains, where there are newer properties on larger lots similar to ours, to be competing. We question why a sale from this area (as opposed to comparable 2) was not included as an indicator of value.

Conclude the rebuttal:

The provided report shows a consecutive set of inconsistencies that lead the reader to believe the opinion of value is unreliable.

Select appropriate but there could be others reasons why the report is unreliable.

a) Analysis of market conditions

b) Failed to report any data to reflect current market conditions.

c) Used questionable data sources

d) Comparable location, land value, utility issues and failure to report external issues that affect value.

e) Data entry errors

f) Unsupported adjustments

h) Did not reconcile the available data and adjusted values.

There are a lot of reasons for concern in the above rebuttal. In fact, if a homeowner could formulate a similar rebuttal, it would be quite a serious situation. Nonetheless, if questions arise over the accuracy of one section that lead to the accuracy of another, coupled with more errors, and so forth then a case can be made for a mis-valuation.

There are some responses from appraisers to certain rebuttal arguments which are questionable.

1) From including a foreclosed sale rather than a standard sale. An unacceptable response is the sale is an "economic foreclosure" or "market foreclosure". The appraiser is stating that due to good market conditions the foreclosure sold for the same amount as a standard sale. Do not accept this argument, as an economic foreclosure requires a robust market. The sale has to sell at 100% of a standard sale to be considered an "economic foreclosure" and not 93% or even 95%. If this foreclosed sale is indeed superior to any other, then a positive adjustment should be applied to the sale price to account for the difference.

2) A frequent question to appraisers is why a particular sale wasn't used. The response is the sale was not pertinent for a particular reason. Check that the reason does not contradict other statements in the report. This problem is remarkably common and deserves another rebuttal. The appraisal is a legal document and it has to be consistent.

3) Beware of the bracketing argument! Sometimes an appraiser states a sale was used to bracket a specific property feature, below the accepted GLA and lot, age, quality of construction or utility if applicable. This is fair enough, but that sale is included for one reason only, being to show the market acceptance of that feature. Typically these sales are included as additional comparables. The inclusion of a sale to bracket an element does not preclude the use of other generally more similar sales. Correct valuation methods dictates the appraiser should include as many sales as it takes to achieve a reliable

valuation. The appraiser should recognize any sales used only for bracketing purposes in the reconciliation.

Appraisers, like other licensed people, are judged by their peers. So if part of the argument consists of elements that show unusual appraisal practice, not be supported by peers, then a strong case for rebuttal already exists.

The Lender is not allowed to order numerous appraisals on the same property. But they are allowed to order a new appraisal, if the first is openly flawed. If any of the below are proven then the appraisal is technically flawed, especially if coupled with other arguments.

Unacceptable Appraisal Practices

The following are considered unacceptable practices for work that submitted to Lenders in today's market. Some will also come up in Federal Law and the Uniform Standards of Professional Appraisal Practice (USPAP). See below.

1) Development of and/or reporting an opinion of market value that is misleading. This word "misleading" is used in the context the subject has to be physically misrepresented in the appraisal report leading to an unsuitable sales selection. Refer to #3.

2) Development of a valuation conclusion that is based, either partially or completely, on the sex, race, color, religion, handicap, national origin, or familial status of either the prospective owners or occupants of the subject property or the present owners or occupants of the properties in the vicinity of the subject property.

3) Misrepresentation of the physical characteristics of the subject property, improvements, or comparable sales. This includes significant problems only.

4) Failure to comment on negative factors with respect to the subject neighborhood, subject property, or proximity of the subject property to adverse influences. This includes failing to report the negative effect of nearby; expressways or any busy two lane road, rail lines, high voltage power lines and adjacent or nearby hazards that would affect the health and safety of the occupants.

5) Failure to adequately analyze and report any current contract of sale, option, offering, or listing of the subject property and the prior sales of the subject property and the comparable sales. The subject's property sales history for the past three years is included in the appraisal report. A similar history for the comparables sales is also included as asked for by professional standards even though many appraisers include a longer sales history.

6) Selection and use of inappropriate comparable sales or the failure to use comparable sales that are locationally and physically the most similar to the subject property.

7) Creation of comparable sales by combining vacant land sales with the contract purchase price of a home that has been built or will be built on the land. The operative word is "creation".

8) Use of comparable sales in the valuation process even though the appraiser has not personally inspected the exterior of the comparable properties by, at least, driving by them.

9) Use of data, particularly comparable sales data provided by parties who have a financial interest in the sale or financing of the subject property without the appraiser's verification of the information from a disinterested source. For example, it would be inappropriate for an appraiser to use comparable sales provided by the real estate broker who is handling the sale of the subject property, unless the appraiser verifies the accuracy of the data provided with another source and makes an independent investigation to determine that the comparable sales provided were the best ones available.

10) Reporting an appraisal in a manner or direction that favors either the cause of the client, or a related party. The opinion of value, the attainment of a specific result, or the occurrence of a subsequent event in order to receiving future assignments is an unallowable practice. In today's market the appraiser will not be informed of the homeowner's opinion of value. The appraiser should not want to know either.

There are many references in the text to "reporting standards". The development of an appraisal has to be consistent with the requirements for appraisal and reporting standards set forth in the Uniform Standards of Professional Appraisal Practice (USPAP). Referring to violations of USPAP as part of a rebuttal should only be considered after consultation with someone that knows about USPAP.

Appraisal Review.

There are two forms of appraisal review, a desk and a field, both are performed by peers.

A desk review is when all data is verified, and each section of the report is checked, together with an overall technical review. The appraiser makes an overall assessment and comments why the appraisal is acceptable, should be revised or otherwise. The appraiser does not include additional sales data in a desk review, and this is one thing that differentiates it from a field review. Remember any additional sales would have to be inspected from the exterior.

A similar function is performed in a field review except the appraiser goes into the field, drives by all the subject, comparable sales and any other deemed relevant. Field reviews are more detailed where the appraiser comments on specific questions to each section of the report under review. A field review includes photo addenda of the subject and sales and a location map.

Desk and field reviews are typically ordered and paid for by the Lender, simply put, on appraisals- *they do not like!* Typically a review is ordered because the value is believed to be too high. A Lender will rarely order a review if the value is too low.

If the situation dictates there is no reason why a homeowner cannot pick up the phone and order a desk or field review from another appraisal company. A homeowner would normally submit a rebuttal before considering peer review. This may have a negative consequence of pitting one appraisal company against the other, but appraisal reviews vary in the same manner as the original appraisal does. There are appraisers who do an objective review and give their best opinion. A good reviewer will find both positive and negative things about an appraisal report. Nothing is, or should not be completely negative. In the case of field reviews some Lenders ask for additional data to support the opinion whether it coincides with the original value or not.

Unfortunately our industry is not perfect and some appraisers will rubber stamp the original appraisal leaving no one the wiser. When ordering a review, like so much in real estate it's a case of buyer beware.

Ordering a desk or field review in a rural area maybe a waste of time. The chances are, there is limited data and the review appraiser will come to the same conclusion.

Things that May Kill The Deal

The matrix that is involved with "What may kill the deal" is larger that it appears. A totally innocent feature or comment in the appraisal report may conflict with information the borrowers' has on their application. This discussion only revolves around problems that exist in homes, that the appraiser will report, and in most cases conflict with Lender guidelines. In some cases Lender guidelines are tied to end investor appraisal guidelines and can be either more or less restrictive.

Things that may kill the deal from an appraisal perspective are usually; the result of legal issues, things may affect the subject's marketability or something the investor may deem an inordinate risk.

Check #28. Before entering into any home loan agreement homeowners take a good look around their property and neighborhood and see if any aspects would conflict with investor concerns. Resolve, or at least think about any possible appraisal issues before paying an application fee. Your loan officer should be able to assist, having the resources to answer questions about possible appraisal issues.

Unnecessary re-inspections to properties are frequent, as a particular aspect was not complete at the time of the initial inspection. Homeowners undertake repairs or renovations and sometimes fail to complete them before the appraisal date leaving a re-inspection necessary. Homeowner might want to remember if a particular room is functional there is typically no problem. If that room, most commonly an unfinished bath, is not functional then the appraiser will have to return when it is, or exclude it from the valuation. No matter the reason a re-inspection always incurs an unnecessary expense. In addition most Lenders have specific guideline to cover such eventualities.

1) Atypical property styles. These include property styles which are atypical not only for a neighborhood but in general. Property styles include geodesic domes, earth berm, homes without sufficient foundation such as houseboats or dockuminiums and properties made with unconventional materials. All these property types are not accepted by most conventional Lenders. See also churches #20.

2) Atypical property types. Any style of property where the property rights might be in question or where there is income. These include adult foster homes, a working farm with a single-family residence, condo hotels, motel conversions and any form of bed and breakfast or boarding house. Signs of a

boarding house would be multiple bedrooms on each floor with a limited number of bathrooms and extensions with multiple bedrooms and not much else. The average family has no reason to have eight or more bedrooms.

Income producing elements are an issue creating a different liability for the investor. Everything has to be allowed, so if the income stream is deemed illegal then this invalidates the income stream. The subject is considered illegal until the income stream stops. This does not include home offices or the "one chair" hair salon in the basement. More specific income producing elements are mentioned below. The income stream must come from an allowable property usage.

The form of ownership known as Co-operatives, are an atypical property and not accepted in mainstream mortgage products. A co-operative comes in many forms but essentially each owner has shares in an "entity" which controls the housing units. That entity could be a LLC, non for profit, in some case shares can be sold readily and in others it's difficult. The words co-operative in some cases is a misnomer as they resemble someone(s) fiefdom as that "entity", needs to be controlled. Clearly the whole process is difficult to underwrite making this an ineligible property type.

3) Second kitchens. A problem for investors as they may be installed illegally and/ or create part of a rentable space. It entirely depends on the investor, so it is a question well worth asking. For the GSE's, Fannie Mae and Freddie Mac, the second kitchen has to be typical for the neighborhood and that is pretty much it. That said any second kitchen cannot be a health and safety issue. The comparable selection should show the commonality of that feature and that it does not impact marketability.

The irony is, in so many cases, a second kitchen is a desirable feature and increases marketability. Nonetheless some Lenders ask for multiple sales especially in the circumstances where the kitchen is technically illegal, yet common to the market and does not form part of a rentable space. The inclusion of too many sales with this feature can mean the end- value is distorted, since the selection has concentrated on the second kitchen and not the subject. Once again sales displaying atypical features should be used as additional sales data.

4) In law-suites. These follow the same principles as second kitchens causing the same concerns for Lenders and end investors alike and are only a problem if illegal. In laws suite usually have to be occupied by a family member and become illegal when not. The set-up has to conform to building code.

5) Additions. Underwriting may require a permit for a recent addition, the appraiser may not ask for it but be prepared to produce them anyway. Verification of the legality of additions is extremely pertinent in today's mortgage industry.

6) Condominium Complexes. Two problems may exist and both create an issue with standard mortgage programs. The first is fatal in the mortgage process. This problem largely exists in vacation markets. The second instance may eliminate the project for financing but exceptions can be applied for.

a) The appraiser will check for the total number of rented units in the project. More than 50% in rental units in a condominium complex is a problem. Do not apply for regular financing if rentals exceed 50%. Why? Just to make this clear, this has nothing to do with renters. One concern is with the potential pricing of units if large numbers of landlords decide to sell.

b) Some complexes include commercial spaces. Usually the commercial and residential sections have separate associations. But if the amount of commercial space in any homeowners association exceeds 20% then another problem exists. Investors are reluctant to have an over influence of commercial while the main purpose of the project is residential. Splitting the associations does not hide from the commercial influence.

Fannie Mae approves all condominium complexes they underwrite mortgages on. The loan officer would check the project to suitable for the loan program.

7) 2-4 Units Multi Family and the Certificate of Zoning Compliance. This certificate may be necessary to prove the number of legal units in a building. Some Lenders do not need it, but homeowners would be wise to clarify the number of rentable units before applying for financing. This certificate could affect the pricing of the loan so it shouldn't be dismissed. On a residential loan it is only possible to finance up to four units after that the property is considered commercial.

8) External Issues. These should not kill any deal; typical external influences include overhead power lines, nuclear power plants, large airports etc. The appraiser needs to find sales with a similar influence. If the influence is significant, like those mentioned, normally this is possible, as other sales in the area would also suffer. Smaller items that create a direct external inadequacy are more problematic. These

would be small brown-fields, silos, abandoned and dilapidated adjacent manufacturing or industrial structures. They are an issue being detrimental to the properties marketability and can be a basis for rejection in underwriting.

9) Manufactured homes are not acceptable collateral to every Lender. Homeowners should disclose to the loan officer immediately if the collateral is a manufactured home, mentioned as some do not. If the Lender does accept manufactured homes, the homeowner's State has to classify these homes as real estate and not personal property. The Lender will require the home and lot(s) to be on one deed.

A manufactured home property rights have to be "fee simple" and not leasehold for mortgage financing. Having a condominium ownership would exclude a manufactured home from conventional financing programs.

In all cases the appraiser has to establish the marketability by the inclusion of other manufactured home sales.

10) Zoning: Certain zoning is going to cause a problem when improvements are single family and the zoning is not. Zoning types include commercial, industrial, any type of manufacturing, exclusive farm use (EFU) and forest commercial (FC) or equivalent. A fundamental part of valuation is that land is used for its best use and not an inferior use. In this case the land would be worth more if improved with what the zoning states rather than a single family home. Therefore the appraiser would note the land and home are not being used for its "highest and best use" which is one of the questions on the first page of every major form. If this is truly the case then this is a huge problem, and the loan is dead. But hopefully this is not the case since the highest and best use analysis also includes one pertinent question. Is it economically possible to improve the land to its current zoning and therefore to its highest and best use? If the market is not showing any signs of desirability to build, for example light manufacturing or a shop, then the current structure of a single family home is the highest and best use and considered acceptable collateral. That said if the zoning differs from the current use, the Lender may refuse the appraisal if the sales in report are all zoned residential. The appraiser needs to clarify the zoning of comparables if this is the case, as the Lender will need to know the differing zoning type is not going to affect future marketability. If this is the case the borrower has the possibility to rebut by going to their municipality and asking for documentation detailing the current zoning. Frequently other zoning types allow for residential usage. This is more common in areas that suffer economically.

11) Legal Non Conforming Property Use. This occurs when the zoning for a property changes and the subject's current legal use is not covered by the new zoning classification and its regulations. Lenders will ask if the house could be re-built in the event of destruction to its current form. This is normally not a problem as municipalities usually have these properties grandfathered in, especially if the property type remains the same. Problems occur when zoning is one use, e.g. multi unit or mixed use and the area is re-zoned to single family with no grandfather clause. In this case the subject is not allowed to be re-built as a multi-unit or whatever. Homeowners and buyers in such circumstances, under typical Lender guidelines will not be able to obtain financing.

12) A high land value may affect the underwriter's decision. High land value has to be typical with all comparables showing a similar value for this to be acceptable. High land value is relative with a small section of Cape Cod Bay at $1.0m plus and may only have $200,000 in improvements, yet if this is typical the loan process is not affected. The appraiser has to show that!

Typical land to improvement ratios would indicate a lot worth $1m would command improvements in excess of $2.5m. If most homes in the neighborhood are such structures then the lot with a $200,000 house would be considered a tear down, as there is a demand for $2.5m plus homes in the market. Lenders will not finance tear downs on a typical loan program and have other loan products for these cases.

There is another instance where a high land value can be problematic. Any given area would start with several large parcels, small farms and for various reasons are sub-divided, either from development or through inheritance. Traditionally large lots were sub-divided by the number of siblings leaving awkward multi-acre parcels. Owners with such parcels, who have hung on to them, while the surrounding area has been developing are going to have problems, especially if there is demand for land to be developed. The appraiser will realize the highest and best use for the land as a small subdivision and not just one home.

13) Multi- Parcel Sites. Lenders are cautious towards properties that have two or more parcels. Multi-parcel sites require all parcels to be on the same deed for typical conventional financing. Each parcel has to be contiguous and the subject's parcel needs to be identified. Surveys are helpful.

14) A house with an adjoining lot on one deed. Homeowners frequently try to finance these separate entities in one mortgage and if they are one deed that is allowable. The problem with this idea is the appraisal! For an appraiser this is two appraisals, firstly valuing the house and then the adjoining lot. If an appraiser is willing to embrace both entities on one appraisal, which some will do, they usually have trouble finding similar sales resulting in a low valuation. The deal goes nowhere!

15) Private Roads. Investors are interested that road access is available for all twelve months, thus insuring marketability. The Lender will want to know who maintains any private roads, if there is some kind of agreement in place for maintenance if the private road is shared with other homeowners. Typically there is no problem with private roads. Some problems usually lie when the road is poor, and seen in new construction in the rural areas where the current access is nothing but a rough in from the main road to the house. Having a private road that is accessible in winter via private ploughs is acceptable.

16) Properties Currently Offered For Sale. For a refinance a Lender will not accept properties currently being marketed. If a homeowner decides to refinance the property while trying to sell, call the real estate agent immediately to remove the sign and the listing. The appraiser should ask the homeowner at the time of inspection if the home has been offered for sale in the prior twelve months. If a homeowner had been trying to sell the property independently they should disclose that, but the appraiser will research any open listing and the sales history for the last three years.

Do not expect the opinion of value to exceed the listing price especially if the property had adequate market exposure. Also most homebuyers would negotiate the listing price.

17) If financing existing rental property, the rental contract has to be provided to the Lender. The rent in the agreement should be paid monthly. This might sound obvious but having rent paid weekly and for periods of three months will suggest a boarding house.

18) Owner of Record. The borrower differing from the owner in public record is not a significant problem, but will slow down the mortgage process. Some homeowners put their property in a LLC, (that has no income) and then file taxes under familial names. The title may need to be transferred as a quit claim deed from the LLC to the borrower. It is an easy legal instrument to obtain.

Property owners should have a will designating an executor. In the event of death property can be sold without waiting for complete resolution of the deceased estate.

19) Life Estates. A life estate is where a property owner has allowed another party to live in a property for the remainder of their lives. The property may or may not be rented for a consistent amount of money. The subject could not be sold during the life of the occupant. Consequently the subject could never be readily marketable in the event of default as it has occupancy issues. Properties with any form of life estates are ineligible property types for mortgage purposes.

20) Log Homes. Lenders still have underwriting issues with traditional log homes, and so they should assuming the subject is a true log home which is a very rustic affair. There is no permanent source of heating and the interior remains largely unfinished. These are the two defining factors, together with the exterior, that make a log home, a log home. Lenders would have problems as there are livability issues. Most homes, however with an exterior of logs are still described as "log homes" by an appraiser no matter the interior finishes and this creates confusion. If every house with an exterior of logs was called a log home then there are some very sophisticated "log homes". Most homes with log exteriors offer the same overall standard of interior finishes to other modern homes so using the description "log home" is a bit misleading especially to underwriters, as some appear trained to be adverse to the concept. In reality properties with log exteriors, modern amenities and architectural features are fashionable and have exceptional marketability.

A classic Log Cabin

Typical country home with a log exterior.

21) Churches. This is another problematic property type. A church converted into a single family home is definitely considered atypical and it's unlikely the neighborhood is dotted with conversions. Homeowners should be aware of any sales in the market area during the last 24 months. If there are none a homeowner should find other examples of unusual homes to show marketability and investigate if any have sold. This will at least gauge how difficult the appraisal process will be. The appraiser will also seek out, so called "odd ball" home sales in the area and use those as indicators of value, if no direct comparables are available, assuming they are of comparable construction and functionally similar. This may or may not be sufficient for the Lender and would be a case by case basis.

On the other hand converted churches into condominiums are becoming increasingly popular and hopefully will not be dismissed by underwriters if marketability can be established. A paragraph on the sales history of eclectic conversions in the market area over the last two years is normally included in the report. Often such projects are well located and an appraiser can use that argument to reinforce the subject's marketability. The condo in a converted church, in a good location, is another fashionable property type.

22) Previous oil well and drill sites. Any active wells and drill sites would immediately dismiss conventional and FHA financing, but what to do when they are no longer active? In all cases the well head should be correctly sealed with no possible access. The ex-drill site may not be within 300ft of the residence. Providing the appraiser with a survey is essential.

Check #29. The process of extracting natural gas known as "fracking" is also a concern for Lenders. Typically the rules are similar for oil well and drill sites, but be knowledgeable about the activity in your area. If "fracking" does exist in the immediate area, a home owner should disclose this and find out, beforehand, if this is going to be a problem.

23) Hazardous building materials and environmental factors. These are various and here are the most common ones.

a) Defective drywall is the most well known and if noticed, the appraiser will ask for an inspection by a professional in this field. The professional (licensed, if applicable if that state and insured) will judge the extent of the damage and define the remediation.

Defective drywall can come from either incorrect installation and mold accumulates or might be a consequence of the product itself. In the early 2000's drywall was imported from China and a quantity of the product was defective. This poor product was basically unstable and after a period of time would react with natural elements. Black blotches would be visible on the drywall, usually within a year or two of installation. The smell is not great either and these fumes are toxic and will serious respiratory problems among other things.

b) Radon. Radon is a natural gas produced by the natural break-down of radium, a radioactive element. For the homeowner the concern is that radon, for instance gets attached to dust particles which are then inhaled. Consequently radon is a noted carcinogen. Radon tests should be conducted if there is a basement as one can imagine that radon permeates from the earth. Remediation takes place if levels exceed those laid out by the EPA. If even radon tests are negative every basements should always be well ventilated as low levels of radon are surprisingly common.

c) Mold. From an appraiser's point of view, this includes anything that looks like mold. Lenders take mold seriously and no mortgage financing can take place until all signs are remediated or released. Once again the appraiser will recommend a mold inspector to assess the problem and solution.

24) Flood Insurance. The cost of flood insurance has risen significantly over recent years and in some cases run to many thousands of dollars.

Check # 30. Before signing a contract check if the property is in a flood zone. If it is buyers should be informed at the possible cost of insurance. If the cost is so high that it affects the property's marketability the appraiser should consider that.

Homeowner's with Unusual Property Types will Face Challenges

Homeowners with atypical properties will have challenges in the appraisal process and should plan for what might lie ahead. Then there are properties that appear to be one thing but are in fact something else. Both appraisers and underwriters should recognize things for what they are. Here are some examples of both.

Underwriters typically look for similar sales to this classic "A" frame in the comparable selection. In this case, however, the property shows more contemporary features and a basic "A" as a point of comparison may be undervaluing this property. The subject is also built-out to the right, on the first and second floors.

Rehabilitated vintage homes may present a problem in finding sales with an equivalent amount of modernization. The property may exceed what the market will bear and be compared to properties of inferior condition leading to a low valuation.

Small two unit properties are being converted back single family homes. If the zoning remains multi-unit the appraiser may consider the subject's highest and best use as such. Multi units would have to sell for higher prices in the market, in which case the appraiser will declare the subject's present use as a single family not the highest and best use. If purchasing a 2-4 unit and converting it back also change the zoning to single family. That way there can be no future problems.

The value of homes by notable architects which are *private* is rarely achieved. The more significant the architect the harder the property is to value. The market would decide what value the architect's name brings and the appraiser would have a tough time supporting it.

A geodesic dome is normally not acceptable collateral in today's market. What is interesting about this home, it has an entrance on the main level, the lower level is most likely finished and the roof is dormered suggesting living space. In other words this has a superior utility to the typical geodesic dome, appears similar to a contemporary home and may well be financeable.

This property is a homestead and perhaps older than one thinks, despite upkeep. The property is basically a two story home with two wrap decks and a portico, yet gives the impression of much grander property. Wrap-around decks add a significant amount of appeal.

Rural Estates on acreage are exceptionally hard to appraise. Sales are commonly 10+ miles from the subject with differing locations that are hard to analyze considering the lack of data. Frequently the appraiser will offer a low contributory value for amenities such as barns, and horse stalls. Typically there is a wide range of adjusted values.

These homes are directly on the waterfront leave not much more than minimal swell created from a weather event for flooding to occur. One really hopes these homes are on a lake.

Property Investments and Things to Avoid

Investing in real estate is similar to any form of investing, know your market and have several reliable data sources.

Modernization and renovations, large or small are completed all the time and every homeowner wonders if their home improvement is going to add value. When looking for answers, probably the worst place is commercial programming. Reality TV with homeowners completing modernization which are later assessed by real estate agents, who tout unachievable returns on small investments are misleading. "We're going to spend $2,500 on and sell this house for $5,000 more" is a mockingly made up quote but the same idea is presented repetitiously. These shows are meant for entertainment purposes only.

For any given project, bear in mind the appraiser is concerned with what increase in value there is. The increase is via how the market reacts to that improvement and we know the market does not react to everything.

A property consists of many individual parts and each contributes a value. The sum total of each part is the total property value. It is invariably the case, the total cost of the house, which comprises of the depreciated existing structure and new(er) improvements exceeds the actual market value. A similar figure is seen in the cost approach, if completed as that number is based off the depreciated value of a replacement home. This figure is also usually higher than the opinion of value. So is the difference between cost and the opinion of value, market reaction? No because of inaccuracies in the cost approach but it is an indication. At the least, it shows the homeowner that not every dollar invested will reappear in the appraiser's opinion of value.

When making significant investments in improvements either via a complete rehabilitation, remodel or modernization, there are ways to get returns. Firstly one needs data. This will provide the investor with sets of parameters showing the minimum and maximum profit. The possible return is within these parameters and what is achievable depends largely on the age and current condition of the subject property.

Condition is thought of in terms of how the subject compares to the average home in the neighborhood. If the home is already in average condition, the chances of any returns would be limited to what a buyer would pay for a home in average condition, when compared to one that has been modernized. If most homes in the area are already in good condition, which then becomes the norm (average), then the chances for any return in simple condition improvements is limited. For example, there is no return in new flooring, if competing houses have the equivalent.

There is some positive light to home improvements. No matter what is completed, the home's overall marketability increases. If the subject is for sale then consider new improvements and modernization as fewer days on the market before a contract comes in. If not, then your home is just that, *your home*, representing security, a need for functionality and the opportunity to show personality. These are all valid reasons homeowner's have for making home improvements, as these factors improve quality of life.

In the market place some home improvements traditionally offer a lower return than others. The finishing of a basement, sun room, decks or energy efficient items are all examples. Home improvements which fall into the "personality" category and are not typical in the neighborhood perform the worst. Appraiser's calls these, "super adequacies", and yield less as they are considered a form of over improvement. If a house is over improved its value is not recognizable via sales of similar homes because there are none. Examples vary on the neighborhood, so unless these items are common the following will contribute only a small fraction to value when compared to cost.

a) Building the largest house in the neighborhood.

b) Additions increasing the gross living area to over and above what is market accepted.

c) Upscale amenities; full scale basketball court, pool houses, built in pools, bowling alleys and complete spas.

d) Superior interior finishes that significantly exceeds homes in the neighborhood which are already considered to be in good condition.

Check # 31. All home improvements are completed in accordance with local building codes. It's common for underwriters to ask for permits on recently completed projects. Improvements may not be recognized by the appraiser otherwise.

Here is a summary of the most popular home improvements. These comments are directed to those who at least would like to try and break even.

Basements

Homeowners should think about doing the work themselves, perhaps gathering a small team, providing beer and food over the week-ends. An appraiser rarely adjusts more than 5-10% of property value for a finished basement, so it helps if costs do not exceed that. That said, finishing the basement maybe necessary to increase functionality and the decision of cost should be based on that rather than a desire for return. Nonetheless think about what is necessary, for example a full bath is unnecessary if no one sleeping down there. As mentioned, adjustments for finished basement are problematic due to the difficulty of extracting data and/or the appraiser's reluctance to do so. This also accounts for their low return.

Attic

Finishing an attic is one of the more profitable investments. Frequently this newly finished area will be added to the gross living area by the appraiser. The larger gross living area will allow for comparison to larger properties and increase value. That is the theory and admittedly it usually works. However whether this increase in value actually occurs depends on the individual attic. Buyer's reactions vary to differing attic spaces. Spaces which are well lit, with skylights or dormers and adequate ceiling height fair better than those that do not. If the building codes are not restrictive, then ensure, at the least, that the new finished attic area has two viable exits in case of emergency.

It's hard to escape the irony that a finished basement, which effectively adds living space, does not contribute much value while a finished attic performing the same function fairs much better. This idiosyncrasy is not easily explained, and maybe a reflection of just how stale some appraisal practice is.

Amenities: Decks and Patios and Gazebos

Each of these features varies in terms of return. A homeowner's goal is to create outdoor living space. Compare the cost of an adequate patio which can be built for $1,500-$3.000 to the cost of a deck, $6,000-$12,000. There are beautiful and expensive decks and patios in the marketplace. But both serve the same function by creating the amenity of outdoor living space. Therefore the patio, on the basis of lower cost is the favored option for anyone wishing to create both an amenity and maybe, if self built, add a little value.

Basement Kitchen

A second kitchen, also known as summer kitchen, is becoming a more popular feature. The value of a second kitchen depends on the neighborhood. In some cases a second kitchen is essential to the buyer, while in other markets it's a superfluous item. Even if the second kitchen does add value the appraiser will have trouble recognizing it.

The most practical way to installing a second kitchen is to wait until the main kitchen needs replacing, and move the old cabinets down stairs. With new countertops, sink and backsplash it will be adequate as these second kitchens are usually meant for heavy duty cooking. It would be surprising if permits are not needed, so check. Typical building codes contain minimum ceiling height, exits, ventilation and correctly installed utilities.

Energy Efficient Items (EEIs)

Solar panels will need cleaning. In areas with high pollen or heavy winters this work has to be accounted for. Systems will not work efficiently if they are not kept clean and not every homeowner is willing to do the work.

The value of energy efficiency is the monthly saving on utility bills, but as indicated possible adjustments for EEIs are only a fraction of the actual cost and probably not even the actual contributory value. Appraisers struggle to find value as it is common to have limited data for these features and the reasons behind low returns.

Additional Bathroom

Adding a bathroom can be a profitable investment. Call an appraiser and ask, very politely, for their opinion. The chances are the bathroom can be built for less than the range in contributory value that is discussed. Markets place good value on a second bathroom and a second bathroom is usually a good investment and where the profit lies. A third bathroom would have less of an impact on value.

Appraisers appear to adjust for baths in a dis-proportionate manner when compared to various property values. On the one hand a property worth $200,000 receives a $5,000 bath adjustment and a $700,000 only $8,000. The most likely cause is lack of data analysis.

Kitchen Upgrades

Appraisers consider appliances as personal property unless they are built-in, but even then will scarcely be recognized in the report. But modern appliances in an up-dated kitchen are a necessity to achieving the best possible sale's price. Even though kitchen appliances and general upgrades have no identifiable value from an appraisal standpoint, they have a huge impact on marketability and that translates into cash. Nonetheless homeowners over spend on kitchens and upgrade to a manner that is above the neighborhood standard. Kitchen improvements are profitable up to a point, so homeowners need to think conservatively if expecting a return. A new stove, backsplash, countertops and re-facing the cabinetry works.

Flooring and Standard of Finishes

How to profit with flooring and standard of finishes requires some market knowledge and a bit of tenacity. After kitchens and bathrooms these features are high on buyers watch lists and also essential to maximizing the property's value on the open market. Buyers are acutely alert to flooring and standards of finishes throughout a home. In this regard buyers consider condition to preside over quality. Nonetheless quality does a play factor and within that, the originality of the finish. Why not use bamboo flooring, over hardwood or dyed cement countertops even quartz instead of the standard granite? Use fashionable items like mosaic tiles and combine that with contemporary features like accents of natural materials. A property needs to attract attention in the marketplace.

As it remains a buyer beware marketplace there some things to preferably avoid.

Buyers Interested in Previously Foreclosed Remodeled Homes

Buyers need to be cautious depending on type of property and the person doing the work. Buyers of previously foreclosed homes "remodeled" should be aware of a couple of things and some will need to be very sharp during the purchasing process.

Find out exactly what is being purchased. Properties are sometimes advertised as being "remodeled" or "rehabbed" and a buyer should find out what that means. Obtain a full list of all repairs and modernizations completed on the property and a cost for each. The "rehabber" should not provide a total cost of the work and leave it at that. Only with a full broken down list can a homebuyer gauge the quality of work completed. Sometimes, selling agents when asked similar questions, simply reply "everything is new" and this is an unacceptable response.

No contracts should be signed until copies of all works orders and permits are given to the buyer. In many ways the willingness of a "rehabber" to provide this information is an indication of their professionalism. Take this list and provide it to the appraiser. By all common technical standards the appraiser will ask for this information anyway, so this request, to the "rehabber" should not be a surprise.

Obtaining copies of all permits reduces the chances of purchasing a house with illegally improved living space. Finished attics are the most frequent example, but it could be a small extension. The appraiser and/or Lender will pick up on that, certainly in today's market, but this means the dream home is not readily financeable, the deal is dead with time and money wasted. Multi-units with finished attics in urban areas need to be looked at very carefully.

The word "rehabbing" and its loose usage in all sorts of verbiage causes confusion in the market place. Here are the definitions of various standards. The word "Renovation" is not included as it only means to "make changes and repair" which is open to interpretation.

Remodeled Home: A property where the interior walls have been removed and rebuilt creating a different and more modern layout. Everything in the home is new, except the exterior shell, sub-flooring and rafters.

Rehabilitated Home: A property where there is no change to the layout but, the interior walls are brought back to the studs and replaced. Exterior siding, windows, electrical, plumbing, and roof and interior finishes are replaced.

Modernized Home: A simple process that does not require new drywall, but new kitchen, baths, flooring, windows, and mechanicals are replaced. Electrical and plumbing are repaired/ updated.

Check #32. First time buyers, remove the emotion when walking into glossy "rehabbed" homes for the first time. There is usually a lot of glitz which is meant to distract. It's a buyer's job to find out what is behind that! Buyers have to know what they are purchasing!

Typically buyers pay too much for "rehabbed" homes. As they normally trade at the high end of the market, buyers need to check their data. To ensure the sales price is not too high, buyers should ask their real estate agent for three lists of homes sales. Each list should include the address, sale date, sale price, and the number of bedrooms and bathrooms.

1) All homes in the "neighborhood" sold in the last twelve months.

2) All so called rehabbed properties in the same area.

3) The most physically and locationally comparable properties modernized or otherwise.

This data will show where the property is trading in the market. The contract price shouldn't be at the very high end of the range in values. Signing a contract with a sales price above market data usually spells trouble is on the way. The appraiser will not be able to support the sales price, technically speaking.

It's understandable if a first time homebuyer, whom many of these homes sell too, does not want to get involved in possible refurbishments. So when negotiating consider the actual cost of improvements since foreclosure. Is the standard of finishes really really worth what has become the sale price? Builder's profits after costs are typically in the range of 20%-30%. It is hard to judge if someone's profit margin is too large, with being a free market, but a home buyer should have an idea of what is typical. Having an idea of the profit a "rehabber" is making, is an important piece of information to have. This can be used as a tool during contract price negotiation. Add the total cost of acquisition (sales price from public sources plus cost to purchase), work orders and permits (which the builder has provided) and selling costs (estimated including real estate fees) to see how this compares to the selling price. The selling costs can be estimated by your real estate agent for a more accurate number. If the profit is too high, refer to work completed, the home could have been merely modernized but the sales price is for a full rehabilitation.

Sales via "For Sale By Owner"

Problems that arise from a "For Sale by Owner", FSBO property, could usually be prevented if all parties had professional representation. The most common problem is a property being over-priced, typically based on what the seller believes the house to be worth. FSBO's sales prices are often higher when compared to property marketed through a real estate agent. It's just a reality and problems on FSBO appraisals occur. If the value is there then fine, but a greater percentage, when compared to an agent's sale, do not meet the sales price. In reality a fraction of appraisers will miss an over-priced FSBO and meet contract price. The error will remain dormant until the borrower applies for refinancing years later, and sees an unexpected low value. In this case if the borrower sought additional professional advice prior to purchasing the outcome might be different. It is, however, a reasonable borrower expectation that the Lender chose a competent appraiser in the first place. The Lender is responsible for their choice.

Advice to the First Time Home Buyer

Many of us spend time thinking about that first home and what it's going to be like. First time home-buyers might want to consider a first home as a step towards a more livable property in the future. The first home might not be perfect and in many respects it only has to be is functional and affordable.

When considering the complexity of today's real estate market, getting to the closing table is a long and emotional process for everyone and for the homebuyer especially so. Buying real estate for the first time is a task, so try to remove emotion from the process. Walk around the apartment chanting, "I will not be emotional" if necessary! Mixing emotion and real estate can lead to irreversible false choices. Just think of the first home in terms of suiting "needs" and not "wants". The moment "wants" are involved the situation becomes emotional. Remember it's just the first home, so any "wants" that end up in the home are a bonus.

Make an effort not to buy too much house and that does not only refer to size! Loan officers tell buyers a possible amount they can loan on. Unfortunately many use this number to base their search, for a new home, from and start looking at larger homes than they can actually afford. Alas, the first mistake, as buyers become attached to what they have seen, and begin to have expectations of that living standard. But there is a difference between what one can borrow and what is affordable. Buyers become disappointed when they have to reconcile with living in a smaller home when they realize the possible loan and affordable amount differ. For those that do not wish to reconcile, remember it is better to live happily in a small house rather than sadly in large one.

Homebuyers that over reach are tempted into thinking in a few years the home will be more affordable. Yes, one might have good career prospects and the possibility of earning more money. Yet if a house is not affordable now, then the chances of it being affordable in the future are slim. The cost of owning property rises throughout the years as the cost to replace items together with real estate taxes and insurances, increases.

Choosing the right partners for the real estate transaction is essential. Loans officers are plentiful, and the company they work for is important. Good loan officers working for good companies sometimes leave and end up working for mediocre ones. There are less experienced loan officers working for good companies, so either way one has to be careful.

The loan officer is the first step to house hunting and not the real estate agent. Choosing a real estate agent is equally important. A good agent is a sales person to get your business, but after that should provide nothing but sufficient information so the buyer can make the right decisions.

Check #33. Who will handle the appraisal process? Ensure the AMC, if applicable, is reputable.

Your Appraiser, Inspection Issues and FHA Inspections

A real estate appraiser is an outside vendor, a complete third party to everything, but at the same time is a representative of the bank. More importantly an appraiser is a licensed person and a homeowner should have some expectations. Homeowners are consumers and can do as they wish within reason, but knowledge of a few industry standards and appraiser etiquette is beneficial, especially in the event of complaint. In addition there are some things to consider before an appraiser arrives for the inspection.

The appraiser is a tradesman of sorts and has numerous problems to solve throughout the day. Nonetheless appraisers need to set expectations. This is the customer service part of their job and need to do it well. When making the appointment the appraiser will set the time, be it specific or a range, disclose that complete access to the whole property is needed, that interior photographs of the living areas and basement will be taken, and if applicable ask the homeowner for access to the attic or crawl space. During this conversation do not be surprised if the appraiser asks a little about the property. How many above grade bedrooms and construction style are common questions, as this information might not be available from online sources. Homeowners please disclose any atypical property features and if there has been a recent addition to the property. Inform the appraiser if a survey or building plans are available for use. This initial discussion is helpful to the appraiser and no doubt everyone wants the process to be as efficient as possible.

The appraiser is there only to see the improvements; construction, floors, walls, ceiling, roofs, kitchens, baths amenities and nothing else. Nonetheless tidying up the house is a good idea. Appraisers also want to access the subject's overall marketability, so it helps if floors are not cluttered. Opening curtains and switching on lights in basements, attics and crawl spaces is helpful.

Hopefully the person at the door will look the part and have in hand camera, measuring tape, clipboard, order, and tax records at the very least. Shorts, coffee and a note pad are not going to work. On the other hand expecting an appraiser to wear business casual is unrealistic. Measuring, moving ladders, looking in attics and crawl spaces are all not suitable activities for this attire.

At the door normally a brief explanation of the inspection process is given including a re-disclosure that interior photographs will be taken. Normally speaking photos of bedrooms are not required but the remainder of the property will be photographed. If the appraiser needs access to the attic, that would be reiterated.

There are few appointment protocols both for homeowner and appraiser.

1) It is not the best idea for homeowners to offer comparables sales. An appraiser is allowed to accept them but only after verifying each one. Most appraisers do not like this practice, however, and prefer to find their own data. Some appraisers might think this is an attempt to influence the sales selection. If there really is a sale the appraiser will not find themselves, then offer it, but mention that is the reason why.

2) Prepare a list of modernization completed on the property in the last three years. If full modernization or rehabilitation has been completed provide extensive details and cost breakdowns to the appraiser.

3) The homeowner should disclose any defects the naked eye cannot see. Disclose the maintenance done to remedy problem areas. Good practice also extends to the appraiser asking the age of major components e.g. roofing, electrical, plumbing and mechanicals.

4) The appraiser should not criticize any aspect of the property.

5) Neither party should discuss the subject's property value, or the possible contributory value of components at anytime, before, during or after the appointment. If the appraiser mentions the subject's value the homeowner should be concerned to the point of calling the loan officer and discussing the situation. Value should not be a concern to the appraiser at this stage. There has been no time to review data collected during the inspection, compare it to sales and reach any conclusions. Conversely homeowners please do not ask appraiser what the property may be worth. The same reasons apply.

It's the homeowner's prerogative to escort an appraiser through the property or not. From the homeowners point of view it's probably best, even though most appraisers like to be left alone. An escort makes sense for larger properties but no matter do not distract the person from working.

Personally speaking some of my renowned blunders were made while listening to a great home-owner story and trying to work at the same time. Most appraisers realize a homeowner or seller is a remarkably useful source of information so typically questions are asked.

Check #34. Try to observe how the appraiser measures the property. A reliable sketch can be a problem for some reason, and mistakes are made even with simple structures. If the subject has complicated angles and the appraiser is using the traditional method of a tape, either offer to assist or do not be surprised when asked to. The tape method remains the most trusted in many eyes. A wide variety of sketch errors exist.

An appraiser measures single family homes from the outside and with market convention a condominium from the inside. The type of measuring device is important. It's not suitable for a house to be measured with a wheel, but acceptable for estimating lot sizes. Electronic measuring devices are popular, yet their accuracy depends on property type and weather conditions. In all cases their accuracy relies on the appraiser's ability to use them correctly. Electronic devices are especially useful when measuring condominiums and contemporary properties. In older properties where exterior walls aren't exactly straight then an electronic device might not be the best idea. Appraisers typically have a variety of measuring devices in their car.

If the homeowner provides either a survey or construction plans, the appraiser still needs to take enough measurements to verify their accuracy. If there's a mistake in the plans that gets translated into the sketch, the appraiser is responsible and not the homeowner. Also neither is the builder, surveyor, deed or online architectural drawing for that matter. The appraiser should verify the GLA with physical data collected at the site. Homeowners inadvertently pass on building plans that were altered at a later date and surveys sometimes have errors, so the appraiser has to be vigilant.

Unfortunately there may come a time when a homeowner has reason to complain about the appraiser's professionalism during the inspection. The complaint is made immediately and not at a later time. Once the report is submitted no complaints are heard or considered. The latent possibility of a homeowner being biased due to the results removes this as an option. Complaints are made to the loan officer and not the AMC if involved. The Lender is the AMC's client and not the homeowner; therefore they cannot answer any complaints or questions for that matter.

Drive by Appraisal?

In today's market, Lenders may well ask appraiser's to call homeowners before conducting this service. Some appraisers believe this is not necessary and not in the scope or work for an exterior appraisal. This is difficult to understand, as a detailed conversation with the homeowner would make the assignment easier to complete and probably more accurate. A disclaimer can be added in the report to the source of pertinent information. This is acceptable appraisal practice assuming the appraiser is careful. Traditionally appraisers when conducting an exterior inspection assume the properties exterior to be reflective of interior condition. This same rule applies today. When a homeowner tells the appraiser the interior is highly updated and the exterior is not reflective of that, the appraiser should make a recommendation to the Lender a full interior appraisal is completed.

FHA Appraisal Inspections

Resolving deferred maintenance is recommended before any inspection, but before an FHA appraisal inspection especially so. FHA inspections have nothing to do with home inspection, and homeowners should not confuse the two. FHA inspections are concerned with the health, safety of its occupant and soundness of the property and are not concerned with cosmetic defects. The main consideration is the item remains functional without impairing health, safety or soundness. Here are the most common conflicts between common property conditions and what FHA will accept.

Health

a) For older properties, built before 1978, peeling paint presents the possibility of lead, therefore FHA will ask for those sections to be addressed. Typical remediation is simply scraping and painting the defective surface.

b) The appraiser reports any signs of mold and exposure to any other health hazards on the property. The appraiser will only describe what is visible during the inspection and provide photos in the report. To the Lender, the appraiser will make a recommendation that a professional, in that field, determine the extent of the problem and any subsequent remediation.

c) Wells and septic systems should have adequate distance between them and the subject property. The minimum distances between a well and septic and home are set forth in local ordinances or in FHA guidelines. Septic systems should not show any signs of seepage and for FHA not be within 75 ft of a well. A well should not be within 10ft of the property line.

d) Oil tanks should not show any leakage. There should not be any underground storage tanks either and if so empty, clean and sealed.

e) In some respects the problem with pests affects structural (soundness) issues more commonly. As it is not typical for a home to have a pest issue, the appraiser will report those that are.

Safety

The appraiser is concerned with anything that might be hazardous. Essentially, if the homeowner considers the problem an issue, then so will the appraiser. These are only the most common noted defects.

a) Any trip hazards, including wiring from appliance to socket or missing floor boards. Excessively uneven walkways are a concern.

b) Overloaded electrical outlets. Single electric outlets with multiple uses can cause an overload. This is easily resolvable.

c) Heating sources with no immediate source of ventilation. This includes forced air units in closets.

d) Unreasonably steep stairways with no railings. Traditionally speaking having no hand rail on a stairway above three steps was a problem for FHA. But this mandatory requirement is no longer in place. Currently it is left to the appraisers' judgment if an unacceptable level of risk exists in the steepness or stability of a stairway. There are still a fragment of appraisers who always ask for the old standard. Stairways to attics and basements should have handrails.

e) Homes with decks without railings above what is walkable. The exterior door on the second floor with no safe passage to the ground, the so called "door to nowhere" will have to be secured so that no accidental exit is possible.

<u>Soundness</u>

The term "soundness" refers to any item that affects the structural integrity of the home. These problems require the opinion of a professional in that specific field.

a) Cracks in any walls, basement defects or bowing supports that are beyond what is typical considering the age of home.

b) A roof that will not last longer than two years. A roof showing excessive curling shingles is in question. Roofs should never be leaking.

c) Windows that would be considered inadequate by all reasonable standards having an identifiable draught. Technically speaking windows with a crack in them are not a problem, but broken windows with an opening will need repair.

Check #35. Ask the loan officer if the Lender requires FHA appraisal standards even on conventional loans. There are some differences between the two but essentially speaking, in today's market, all Lenders are concerned with health, safety and soundness.

If there are concerns consult with a loan officer asking if it's sensible to proceed without resolving the issue first. Either way any FHA issues will have to be resolved before the loan closes. The appraiser will state what the problems are in the report, and what has to be done. A re-inspection will occur and this incurs an expense.

In cases where a professional opinion is required, an inspector will be called in and the report will be sent to the Lender for further consideration.

USDA Rural Housing

If applying for USDA rural housing development loan the appraisal report follows all the same rules as FHA. A USDA loan is a good product for those who are eligible. The subject is usually rural, but not always.

Home Inspectors

Home inspectors are licensed in most States. A home inspector should explain their role and what they do for a home buyer. It appears a portion of home inspectors arrive at the property and merely say, "I am here for the home inspection", not pointing out what is going happen. A home inspection is meant to inform the buyer of the condition of the property and typically the inspector will compile a report based on 20-30 points with sub classes. When leaving they describe the deferred maintenance and some ways to remedy them with cautionary notes. What some home inspectors don't say is that most re-sale homes have some problems. If the problems are typical for a house of that age, is a good question to ask.

The home inspection is meant to inform the home buyer as much about the house as possible. The home inspection report is not meant to be a laundry list of repairs for the seller. The seller, however, should still remedy anything that is reasonable and especially any health, safety or soundness issues. What is not reasonable is asking the seller to repair minor deferred maintenance previously disclosed prior to contract signing. Every home buyer should have a home inspection.

Have AMC's Been Good for the Industry?

Whether AMC's have been beneficial for the appraisal industry, should not be a concern for the average consumer going about their normal course of business. Unfortunately in today's market this is not the case. One should take a deep interest in who is handling the appraisal process as some AMC's produce a better product than others!

AMC stands for Appraisal Management Company and the majority of Lenders use their services to manage the appraisal process. The Wall Street Reform and Consumer Protection Act (Frank Dodd) made it clear there has to be some separation between Lender and Appraiser. As a result of this legislation AMC's flourished and dominate the industry today. Lenders do not have to use AMC's and have choices, for example they can set up an independent panel of verified appraisers. There are also other smaller acceptable platforms which are popular with smaller Lenders. But in most cases Lenders choose not to set up panels due to cost and are reluctant to use the alternatives as there are limited options for quality control.

The vast majority of appraisals however, are ordered through AMC's. Sadly there are some companies that lack what it takes to deliver a quality product on a consistent basis. Yes, some of the low quality products are tied to the same set of AMC's. But apart from that, it is typically the circumstances the appraisal is ordered under that will play the largest role in the quality of the report.

Lenders contract AMC's to provide appraisal management services for them. They are responsible for the ordering, assigning and billing of appraisals. This is the definition of an AMC.

> *"in connection with valuing properties collateralizing mortgage loans or mortgages incorporated into a securitization, any external third party authorized either by a creditor of a consumer credit transaction secured by a consumer's principal dwelling or by an underwriter of or other principal in the secondary mortgage markets."*

The AMC' industry is similar to any other and exists in many forms. They play an essential role in the appraisal process and are responsible for selecting the appraiser. The final responsibility, however, of who that appraiser is still lies with the Lender.

The appraisal management industry shows an array of services with some business models working better than others. Some AMC's pay attention to quality and also pay higher fees to appraisers, while others fail on one or both of these points. Here is the Appraisal Management Industry summarized.

Type "A" offers an acceptable service. In this model the AMC has an understanding of what the appraiser has to do. The appraiser will have the opportunity to negotiate fees but for the typical assignment offered a fair fee.

This model differentiates itself in the way the AMC charges its fees. The fees due are clearly set and do not vary from assignment to assignment. Equally as important, is the report is read and reviewed by a peer and the AMC also offers quality vendor servicing. Lastly invoices are settled promptly. Type A is the only acceptable form of AMC in the marketplace.

Then there is Type "B", where some of the causes for concern lie. There is a surprising amount of AMC's that fall into this bracket and there are some hallmarks.

a) There is limited ability for the appraiser to negotiate fees.

b) The appraiser can either set his own fee or accept what is offered. But, whatever the difference between what the homeowner has paid and what an appraiser is willing (has) to accept is profit for the AMC. So in these cases the fees due to the AMC are not clearly defined. In some instances the split between AMC and appraiser is as high as 70/30. I am not familiar with any other industry that doesn't have to inform the consumer what its fees will be, in advance. This raises questions as to whether each homeowner is given the same fair access to a quality of appraisal.

c) Fee will go up for a complex property and only a portion is passed on to the appraiser for additional work.

d) Rely partially or exclusively on technology based quality control.

e) May or may not settle appraisers invoices promptly.

Type is "C" is similar to Type "B" but substandard. There is an extreme amount of money to be made with an AMC and the industry has attracted many a "businessman". There are a few notable names in this bracket, but AMCs like this frequently fail, as when the product wanes so does the Lender's enthusiasm for this company. These companies have traits. AMC fail on a frequent basis and to date owe appraisers literally tens of millions of dollars.

a) Predominate amount of business comes from one Lender.

a) High fee to the borrower and low fees to the Appraiser.

b) No room for the appraiser to negotiate with set fees on single and complex properties.

c) Payments to appraisers are tardy.

d) Poor quality control.

e) Sparse or no vendor service.

This just a summary and these business models blend but from this information homeowners have an idea with whom they should be working with.

Some appraisers are happy or simply have to work for AMC's types B and C. It could be that they are great numbers geeks and willing to plow along. But in some cases these are the only companies that accepts the appraiser work.

Some appraisals are more equal than others and a number of factors will dictate what kind of scrutiny the file is subjected to. Who the Lender is, complexity and ebbs and flow in the business cycle, all account for the amount of quality control a report receives.

Apart from Type A which predominately rely on peer review, most AMC's use some kind of technology as the core part of quality control. This technology is based on a number of factors. Usually large variances in sales data, adjusted values and distances of sales (when compared to the area) are all reasons for flagging a report. It is possible variances are a signal for further quality control but far from a guarantee. In cases where there is little variance, the basic facts will be checked within a report and then sent along to the Lender. As variance has nothing to do with quality this could still mean that a faulty report is delivered to the Lender.

After the appraisal report leaves the AMC it will be reviewed by the Lender. The type and/or lack of review at the AMC can cause questions from the underwriter to the appraiser. From a homeowners perspective this may mean it takes longer to close the loan.

The mortgage appraisal industry is a market but not a true market. It is highly influenced by major players, being both the Lenders and the AMC's they nominate. It is typical for Lenders in today's market to use several AMC's and that is a good thing in most ways. But some AMC's mostly represent one large Lender which have large volumes of business, and can easily dictate a fee structure on available work. It only takes a few companies following the same idea and fees are so depressed that a true market ceases to exist. For some appraisers the problem is exacerbated by banks and mortgage companies being regional so there might not be a wide base of Lenders able to offer steady work. Therefore the appraiser is forced to work for a mediocre AMC with similar fees. Most appraisers do try and build their business model away from needing the run of the mill AMC, but it's just a reality some work will come from this direction, at least for a period of time.

Check #36. It is important to ask your loan officer what is the total appraisal fee, and how much of that is being paid to the appraiser. Does this split make sense and does it seems fair? Ask the loan officer if their mortgage company uses several AMC's or just one. If more than one, is there a choice?

Appraisers are supposed to be paid what is termed a "customary and reasonable fee" (C&R) for their work. This was a Federal response to protect appraisers from low fees. This standard has not worked as each and every day appraisers are being asked to complete work at minimum fees. A C&R fee was supposed to be based off a survey of local fees to determine what is deemed customary and reasonable. How valid can these statistics be since a portion of appraisers have no choice but to accept low fees? Are appraisers to understand this means, "Yes" it is customary to pay low fees and since it is customary the low fee is also deemed reasonable? What is an appraiser supposed to do, receive an order for $200 and complain immediately about C&R fee or complete and complain later. To date Alabama is the only State to create a plausible system for this to work and the only other acknowledgment of "C&R", via by the States, is asking for appraisers to disclose their fee within the body of the report. This only helps the borrower since the appraisal report is already completed for that fee. "C&R" a good idea but so far had little impact on the pricing of appraisals.

States are beginning to legislate rules and regulations surrounding AMC's and thirty plus have already done so, with new additions and amendments to existing law continuous. In most cases however, the regulations are simple, being recently put in place, and need expanding and detailing. Note. Utah asks for the disclosure in the report of both the appraiser and AMC fee.

A few AMC's have realized the criticism when it comes to fees, what is retained by the AMC and the actual portion paid to the appraiser. Some AMC's clearly ask appraisers to state their own fee which is an excellent idea, theoretically. The consequence is that an AMC has a panel of appraisers who offer services within a wide range of prices, for example for a single family home from $200-$500. This leaves some questions.

1) An AMC knows how much work goes into an appraisal. So why would they consider an appraiser with highly discounted fees? A plausible explanation would be to increase profitability but at whose expenses?

2) Some AMC's have large numbers of appraisers available for work on their books, and in cases upwards of 20,000 approved vendors. From those appraisers, they deemed qualified, they may use only 20%-25% on a regular basis. Why are they using so few, are all the rest so terrible and if so, why are they able to stay registered? AMC's state that they include proximity and performance in the appraiser selection but this still does not explain why so many are not considered. One possible reason is the remainder offer a higher quality of service and expect to be compensated for it.

At the end of the day Lenders are responsible for the AMC they choose.

Improving our Industry

If the borrower is aware of all the imperfections and pitfalls in an appraisal report and the lending industry is content, perhaps there is no problem and the point is mute. But for some homeowners this is not the case, with appraisal report in hand, it's evident they are embroiled in a dysfunctional industry. Does the industry have the will or desire to do better, who knows? The GSE's, Fannie Mae and Freddie Mac are certainly trying everything they can and produce continual updates, most minor but some major. The Federal Housing Administration (FHA), has incorporated their own handbooks and numerous updates into one usable document. The States have been tightening on appraiser qualifications and passing legalization on AMC's, even though tardily. On another level the Appraiser Qualification Board (AQB) states that all future appraisers need a college degree. So for those that sit and wonder, something is happening. However, all this work will not truly succeed when such a disconnect exists between Lender and Appraiser. Since it's the Lender that orders the appraisal, initiatives might start from that direction. Perhaps paying greater attention to the appraisal process and especially who is handling it. Admittedly there are Lenders who are somewhat proactive but generally the industry might be inspired to do so, if borrowers become more vocative about the quality of their appraisal report. The mortgage appraisal industry needs to serve the public in a better manner. Be it appraiser A or B, the consumer should have a similar expectation in respect to report quality. Work would have to be done on all sides to achieve that.

The message from the GSE's is largely the same, who strive for greater consistency, yet the government has made a big effort to separate Lenders and Appraisers. Values increased rapidly before the recession and it was felt there was collusion. More often than not, however, there was none, Lenders were merely pressuring appraisers to come up with values, there is a difference. Nonetheless this problem contributed to the housing bubble and its consequent crash, there is no doubt. The Wall Street Reform and Consumer Protection Act (Frank Dodd) is also responsible for separating the mortgage and appraisal industries and it worked. The wall made, however was so high, Lenders and the average field appraiser are left with no understanding of each other's problems as most sit on either side of an AMC. Certainly, in today's market, there is limited input from the appraiser, who is the producer of this product, in almost all quarters. In the mortgage industry the appraisal report in a "product".

Would it be appropriate for an AMC to own any of the appraisals companies they use as vendors? Most would say no as it would be hard to imagine that, on occasion, a conflict of interest wouldn't exist. So why does this same principle not apply to the various Lenders that have a financial interests in the AMC's?

Problems for the Appraiser

Overall, appraisers should try and improve the quality of report writing as one of the cornerstones to improving the industry. The reader needs to be better informed on the analysis of current markets, explanation of adjustments and reconciliation, among other things. With such points included, the average amount of time spent to complete a satisfactory appraisal, is at least eight hours. Compare this with the average appraisal fee, then current compensation levels are an issue. Appraisers who report correctly realize the time spent to complete assignments, when compared to the average fee makes for poor economics.

How can the next generation of appraisers be trained, if there is insufficient income for the current? The average age in the current work force is in the mid fifties, so the industry needs a next generation. Appraiser starts out on split fee basis, so current sets of low fees hinder the profession as a whole. Higher fees would make it more viable for new blood to enter the industry. The appraisal industry is starved of new talent. The cost of apprenticeship is high, for the apprentice and mentor alike. An apprentice needs to be escorted from property to property. Overall the industry needs at least a 30% increase in fees, to keep it modestly sustainable. In many ways the key word is sustainable and one idea is from, the Appraiser Qualification Board (AQB) asking future appraisers to have a college degree. This is a good idea as a degree teaches critical thinking, but no college graduate, considering their expenses, would ever want to enter the appraisal industry simply because it wouldn't be economically viable.

This is not a call for the current price of an appraisal report to rise by 30%. The appraiser has not seen a pay increase in 8 years yet during the same time period the Lenders have seen significant price increases, 100%, on average in the cost of appraisal reports. These additional costs have been passed onto the borrower and the difference is largely going to the AMC's. A borrower paying $550+ for a report is typical in today's market, while the field appraiser can receive only $250. There can be no possible good reason why the AMC needs to charge a $300 handling fee and why do some Lenders allow it? In some case they allow it because they have a financial interest in the AMC, so the money goes back to the parent anyway. At least that is understandable, despite being wrong, but for others it's bewildering. On the whole Lenders have to be considerably more discerning on what happens to the appraisal fee. After all, this is someone else's money!

This means the money to improve the appraisal report already largely exists. The resources just have to be pushed away from the AMC's and towards the appraiser.

Improving Appraiser Education

The work appraiser do involves the public and this is why they are licensed. To renew a license the State asks for continuing education. The continuing education may be taken; either exclusively online, part online and through in classes given by an instructor. The standard of continuing education is mediocre either online or through classes. What is true for most continuing education classes is the material could be covered in a fraction of the time. The live classes are the most disappointing with instructors spending too much time justifying why they are qualified to teach the class and on other trivial matters. They arrive with insufficient material and little to keep the audience from getting distracted. Online classes are convenient but technology further allows appraisers to lead an isolated life which is not a good thing. Online classes remove the peer interaction they would have received at a live class.

Mentorships

After basic education and passing an exam to enter the field, an appraiser usually starts their career working in an appraisal shop putting all the theoretical work into practice. They are guided on how to deal with standard industry problems from a mentor. But, exactly who is this mentor? Is the mentor teaching a set of recognizable appraisal standards or something else? Reviewers have conversations with appraisers over technical issues only to find this is how the appraiser was taught and practicing this way for many years. If a mentor passes down an incorrect opinion the error becomes systemic and practically impossible to remove. With practical experience being such an intrinsic part of the appraiser's education, mentors should have an additional educational requirement to bring an apprentice into the industry.

Appraisers could do more for themselves. Technology does allow appraisers to share ideas and information. Appraisers could even contribute data on market trends, share data on adjustments and mentor each other in their own areas. This would increase the profitability per appraisal report while increasing quality.

Problems at AMC's and Lenders

The mortgage industry needs to work on standards of education, in the same way appraisers do, in respect to appraisals at least. No one is asking for loan officers and those few underwriters that still look at appraisals to understand everything. But these professionals should know some important elements to valuation. Loan officers should know enough, not to waste everyone's time accepting a loan application when there will be appraisals issues. Similarly underwriters need to learn enough about appraisal theory to know what contributes to value, if that remains a part of their job.

If you ask a field appraiser, what is the biggest problem in their daily work life, the response would be the number of revisions requests they receive. Changes to the report could be from the course of the transaction or through stipulations (aka stips) placed on appraisals. Stipulations are a condition for the appraiser to complete before the appraisal is accepted. These could be from the Lender or AMC, as the appraisal has to be acceptable to both. The AMC would have quality control in terms of a technical review and acceptable format only, while the Lender may have an actual question on valuation. Then there are changes to the sales price, changes to/or the inclusion of seller concessions, and if the borrower disputes the file, are all reasons for additional work. These are examples of why a report can be changed and all can be requested on the same file. As a file is already revised many times there is no room for superfluous stipulations that distract appraisers from what they should be doing. To complicate matters underwriter's requests are often poorly explained and sometimes not even in the appraiser's scope of work. Therefore appraiser responses to questions are frequently inadequate which serves nothing but to frustrate the underwriter. It would make sense for the appraiser to respect the stipulation in a more formal manner, when they are valid and point out politely with reasoning when they are not.

During the mortgage process, borrowers provide all their private information and it's up to Lenders to keep it that way. Unfortunately the handling of this information remains casual, despite efforts on the Federal level is keep it confidential. For example Lenders forward a copy of the purchase contract to the appraiser for their review. These contracts, at least remarkably often, include a copy of the borrowers earnest money check. The Lender is not only providing banking information of that borrower to the appraiser but to anyone at the AMC. Other personal information also gets attached to contracts, either by error or otherwise, including W2s and sections of credit reports. This is startling common. At AMC's processors, reviewers and managers can all see the same file. The system is open to unscrupulous behavior and Lenders need to review their current policies on the handling of borrower's private information.

Check #37. Potential borrowers always provide a cashier's check for earnest money. If a personal check is provided one never knows who will see your bank information. When emailing documents to Lenders, each should have their own file. The Lender is unlikely to separate several documents that are included in one file.

Some in the industry have taken to outsourcing a part of quality control to other countries. It's difficult to see any possible wisdom in this. This kind of quality control is supposed to be "basic" but if that is the case there is technology to deal with it. Therefore what are these personnel checking? Most likely a more extensive form of quality control takes place leaving the open question, is this person qualified?

Other Parties that Need Improvement

The availability of data from public sources, to complete appraisals still has a long way to go. These are important points of reference enabling the appraiser of check if a sale is comparable. Those Townships, who do not have all their information up to date and online, should think about the economic benefits of doing so. How fair are valuations if information is not accurate or not available? If a homeowner doesn't get a fair report then the chances of that family achieving their goals is minimized.

Real estate agents have to sell houses and appraisers have to appraise the house when it sells. There are many ways a real estate agent can help.

a) If a property sells before the listing begins, create an online profile nonetheless and upload any information. Some real estate agents at this point just write "Sold before processing". This helps the appraiser only partially as there is no reference to condition. Adding some detail will save a call from the appraiser.

b) Seller concessions are sometimes forgotten when closing out a listing. This is important information to an appraiser. Add notes if the price was negotiated to include an improvement or personal items, furniture for example.

c) Measure rooms accurately and be descriptive on listing sheets. Perhaps add notes of what those amazing updates were when closing out the listing without spending too much time. Simply write, *"Roof 2012, furnace and hot water heater 2010, all new floors except baths and kitchen updated in 2008 and 2011 respectively"*.

d) Understand more about what makes a property financeable and what issues within a property might affect the appraisal process, its marketability and end valuation. A simple example: A roof that needs replacing will need to be completed before closing.

To express the idea the appraiser is plagued with a lot of unnecessary work and problems. Here is a list of the not so sensible things Lenders and AMCs ask appraisers to do. This list is a sampling and included to give the reader an idea of the appraiser's daily problems. One might call is a *"Ridiculist"*. As they are all irritating it hard to access a particular order.

1) AMCs asking an appraiser to complete an appraisal report after 48 hours from inspection even though they can see circumstances do not allow for that.

2) AMC set fees with the appraiser having limited options for pricing due to the assignment complexity.

3) Fannie Mae's instructions and implementation of the market condition report (MCR).

4) Asking for data in the market conditions report to match the data in the neighborhood analysis (inventory) section when these are two differing datasets.

5) Lenders asking appraisers to do things they cannot do, for example to appraise two separate entities on one appraisal.

6) Asking for sales that are only meant to support the marketability of one specific feature when it is obvious that feature would increase marketability.

7) Excessive and/or unwarranted appraisal stipulations and assignment conditions either from the AMC or Lender.

8) Asking for property types such as "site condominiums", basically a detached single family home to be completed on a condominium form.

9) Asking for additional comments on geographic competency, when every appraisal already includes this statement on the certification pages, a part of every appraisal form.

10) Out-dated comments. For example, comments on variances between the opinion of value and predominate value for that neighborhood when similar properties are included as comparables which show that other properties with a similar value range exist.

Conversely appraisers make some questionable choices and are able to do a few mind boggling things themselves. So this is our *"Ridiculist"*.

1) Not adjusting for an aspect to a property when all data indicates one is due.

2) Not being flexible in the scope of work when recognizing more data needs to be analyzed to form an opinion of value.

3) Leaving inconsistencies in a report or rebuttal and wonder why it is a problem for the homeowner and Lender.

4) Placing information, data or commentary, which has a recognized field within the appraisal form, in a completely different section.

5) Stating an aspect of a property does not affect marketability when the majority of peers in the same market say it does.

6) Blanket and canned comments. Blanket comments are a one liner to cover a multitude of variances within the grid. A canned comment usually belongs to a series of comments and the appraiser checks those that apply to the subject property. Neither is informative.

Additionally unhelpful is submitting report in an unrecognized grammatical format with the first letter of each word capitalized. Reports written in all capitals are hard to read, yet the appraiser thinks this helps.

7) Out-of-date stock comments. These are comments in the addenda helping to explain a situation for a particular appraisal but not relevant to the current assignment. For example, stating in the scope or work that crawls spaces are not inspected where the Lender is asking for a FHA inspection.

8) Including long convoluted sentences that conflict in interpretation and meaning which do not make sense to the reader. One might call this "appraisalese", it's not translatable and not helpful.

9) When an appraiser is statistically in error, supported with data, and the report states their opinion is backed by their independence as an appraiser. Appraisers should not be afraid to show humility.

10) Not using mapping software to show all locations of the subject and submitting a copy of map with sticky notes.

The Lender/Appraiser relationship needs to be re-thought seeming not beneficial to anyone. Frank – Dodd is all well and wonderful but under current situations Lenders should have an inherent interest in what appraisers have to say. After all Lenders have only one interest, to get the best possible collateral valuation the market can provide. If these groups were to ever meet the result would be constructive. Observers would remark this would be a key element to improving the industry. In addition the interaction appraisers receive with peers would be beneficial and lead to a greater understanding of the end clients needs. Appraisers would have a platform to bring up cost issues and would realize this opportunity would create an opportunity to improve their lives and profession. Examples of standard meeting agenda items could be the performance of their intermediary, the AMC. If a Lender had a specific problem, a specialist in that field could do a presentation on the topic. The independence of appraisers would not be affected with the presenter being from a third party, assumed a peer.

A case on why appraisal report quality needs to improve has been made to the homeowner, but not to completely to the Lender. The final argument is that Lenders are slowly becoming more liable for the appraisal reports they use to support collateral in the mortgages they re-sell. The appraisal report is a vulnerable part of a loan if something goes wrong, or if scrutinized from the end investor. In many ways, in today's market it's easier than ever before to cite a deficient appraisal. A professional eye will use common basic deficiencies to build a case for inadequate reporting standards and after that normal recourse paths will follow.

Disclosures

The text above relates to the mortgage industry as a whole.

There are references to what appraiser may or not do. All the references and noted problems are common and relate to real incidents and a compilation of opinions.

USPAP. Standing for Uniform Standards of Professional Appraisal Practice is basically the appraiser's guidebook on performing an appraisal in a correct manner. In that case why has there been little reference to USPAP in the text? Any professional appraiser will say that some of the appraisal issues listed in the text are contradictions to USPAP. Only a professional can cite a violation of USPAP, however after knowing all the facts. Referencing each problem to USPAP would be pointless for the average reader. If a serious problem exists then the chances are it'll conflict with USPAP anyway.

There are references to what an Appraisal Management Company may or may not do. The utmost has been done to clarify the variances in service across the industry, despite the categorization , this is meant is to simplify the industry for homeowners but is stood by.

This text is written by a real estate appraiser but is also a collection of opinions and summary of thoughts by peers. These notes are also based on observation and consideration after experiencing the industry from most sides; real estate agent, staff appraiser, independent appraiser, various capacities of review appraiser and collateral review underwriter.

Real estate in all its ways creates personal wealth. A significant amount of life stems from the ability to finance property and its relative ease is almost unique to the continental United States. There are countries where property rights are hard to obtain therefore nothing should be taken for granted and we as a society should recognize that.

Contact: Yourrestateappraisal@gmail.com

Thank you Susan and Grace. All SPC brothers be happy.

© Adrian Watts 2013.

CPSIA information can be obtained at www.ICGtesting.com
Printed in the USA
LVOW09s1556160314

377624LV00023B/641/P